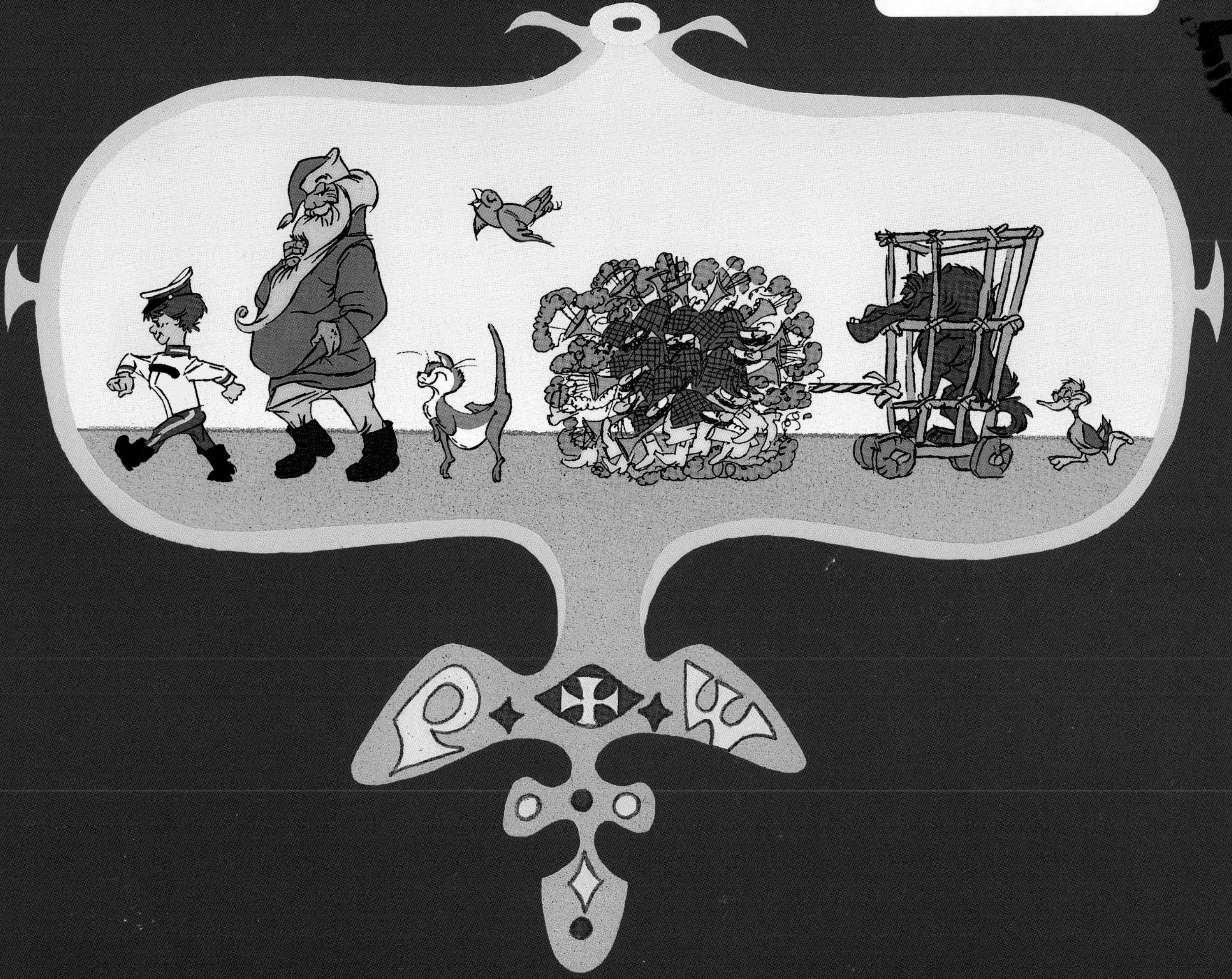

Chuck Jones

Peter and the Wolf

Characters & Illustrations by

Chuck Jones

Written by

GEORGE DAUGHERTY & JANIS DIAMOND

Based on the Production Created by

GEORGE DAUGHERTY

WARNER BOOKS

A Time Warner Company

Chuck Jones'

Peter and the Wolf

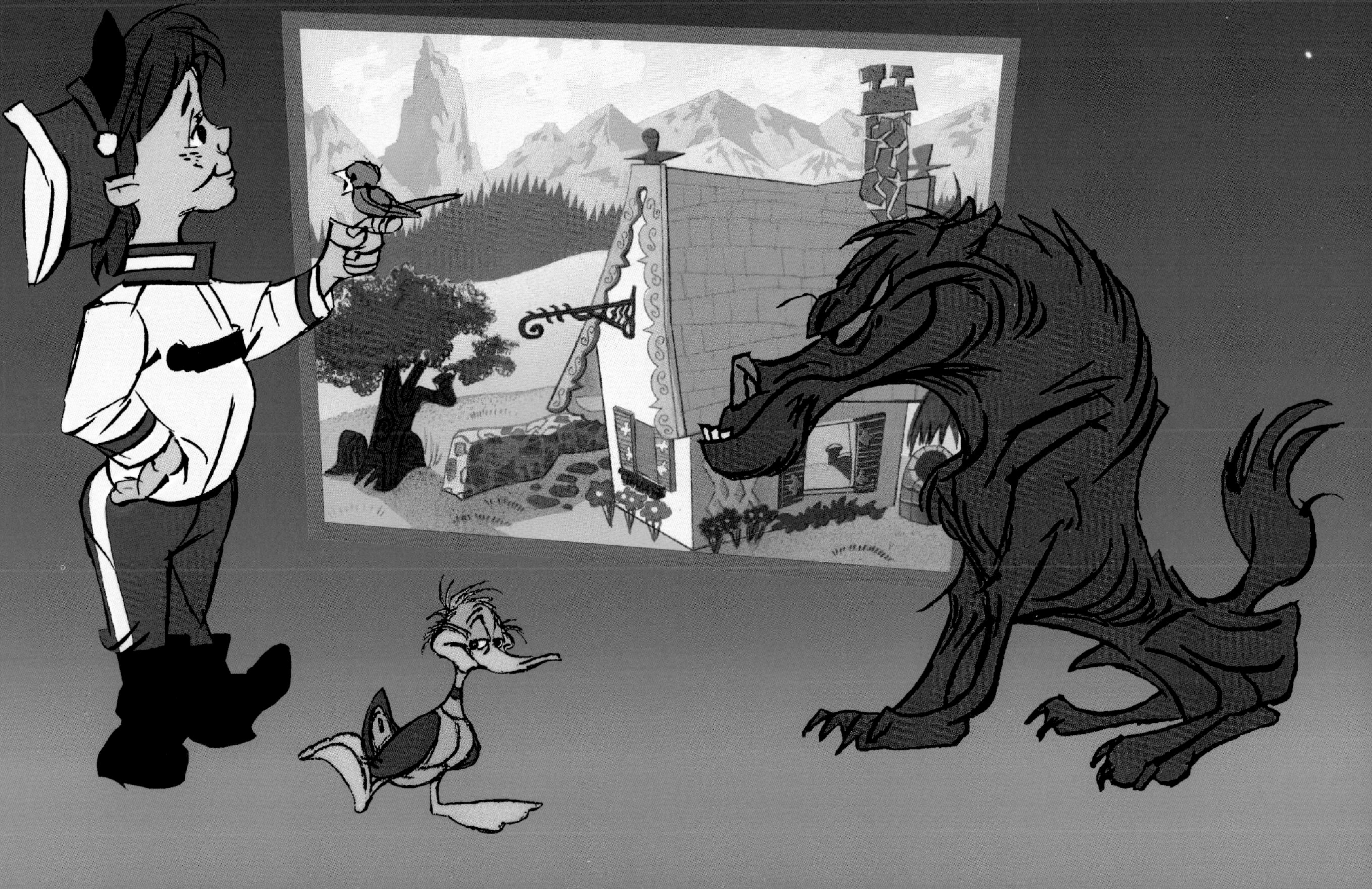

Art direction and book design by Liney Li.
Background designs by Bill Kroyer
Production and concept created by George Daugherty
Project Co-Executive Producer: David Ka Lik Wong
*Based Upon **Peter and the Wolf** composed by Sergei Prokofiev*

Warner Books, Inc., 1271 Avenue of the Americas, New York, NY 10020
Ⓦ A Time Warner Company

Printed in the United States of America
First Printing: November 1994
10 9 8 7 6 5 4 3 2 1
ISBN: 0-446-51894-8
LC: 94-61124

Dedicated to Sergei Prokofiev

(1891–1953)

whose magical music has fired

so many imaginations, and inspired so many

children—of all ages—

to conquer their own wolves.

INTRODUCTION & ACKNOWLEDGMENTS

by George Daugherty

By the time I was 12 years old, I had decided that I wanted to be a conductor. And a writer. And a filmmaker. And, depending on the day of the week, any of about three dozen other creative careers (except on those days that I wanted to be a fireman or a cowboy or an astronaut).

But seeing that being a conductor was way up there on my list, I decided I needed an orchestra. It never occurred to me that the wonderful little town where I had lived my whole life (Pendleton, Indiana, population then 1,900) didn't have an orchestra. Or even a string program in the schools. Being just an ordinary kid who loved music a lot, those obvious limitations didn't cross my mind.

Instead, I decided to stage my own concert, with a gaggle of my junior high band buddies commandeered and bribed into serving as my symphonic ensemble.

And the musical victim? Prokofiev's *Peter and the Wolf,* which had captivated me ever since I heard it as a six-year-old on one of Leonard Bernstein's famous Young People's Concert broadcasts.

It also didn't occur to me that I could have asked my mom and dad to buy the music for me. Instead, I put my seven years of piano lessons to good use, listened over and over to the record, and plunked out my own arrangement of *Peter and the Wolf.* Of course, since I had no string players in my "orchestra," I had to make a few minor adjustments. As I recall, Peter's enchanting theme was played by a bunch of 11- and 12-year-olds honking on their saxophones, in lieu of the majestic string section envisioned by Prokofiev.

Nevertheless, this ad hoc *Peter and the Wolf* took place in June 1967, next to, quite appropriately, the duck pond in Pendleton's beautiful Falls Park, with wonderfully magical narration provided by the town's beloved 70-year-old librarian Mary Ahrens. The whole performance, which was undoubtedly musically hard on the ear, was enthusiastically cheered on by half the town. That we got through it at all was probably a miracle in itself, but for me, it is a cherished memory that will always hold as fond a place in my heart as my conducting debuts, many years later, at The Munich State Opera House, American Ballet Theatre, or The Hollywood Bowl.

In 1994, 27 years later, comes an equally miraculous *Peter and the Wolf,* now brought to life as an animated CD-ROM interactive production, an audio album, and as you know by now, the book you are holding in your very hands, which my wonderful co-author, Janis Diamond, and I have taken such pleasure in writing.

And this time around, nobody will have to dodge a barrage of screaming saxophones.

Somehow, it seems all too fitting that this entire new project was spawned as an interactive CD-ROM, for I think that *Peter and the Wolf* itself was probably the original interactive story. After all, so many diverse and celebrated narrators have lent their own individual interpretations and personalities to Prokofiev's wonderful tale ever since it was created in

1936, and audiences and listeners everywhere have painted their own unique characters and backgrounds, right in their minds. Truly interactive.

Nonetheless, with our new *Peter and the Wolf*, we all feel, quite proudly, that the trappings are incredibly perfect, with delightfully witty, masterful performances by Kirstie Alley, Lloyd Bridges, and that 10-year-old scene-stealer Ross Malinger as Peter; breathtaking backgrounds and layouts devised by Bill Kroyer; a truly fantastic book design by Liney Li; a stellar musical performance by The Time Warner Symphony Orchestra; and serving as the lightning rod for all of this, the inimitable, unforgettable characters and artistry of Chuck Jones, whose genius started this entire creative snowball rolling down the side of the Matterhorn, right into Peter's peaceful meadow.

I've always loved the work of Chuck Jones. His inspired masterpieces starring Bugs Bunny, Daffy Duck, the Road Runner, Wile E. Coyote, and the rest of his indefatigable, insouciant, and oftentimes irreverent ensemble have been a vital part of my life—and the lives of so many millions—as long as I can remember. And, as I've matured into something akin to adulthood, they've taken on a whole new, marvelously sophisticated patina.

Chuck Jones is an American classic, and an American original. And I, for one (although I know I am not alone in this thought) think that his body of work and his unique gifts place him on a very short list of other American masters whose artistry, whose images, and whose words have moved us and delighted us in a way that only true genius can—geniuses like Frank Capra, Charlie Chaplin, Mark Twain, Will Rogers—and Chuck Jones.

Happily, for all of us, Chuck is still in the absolute prime of his creative spirit, and has returned to Warner Bros., where he is mischievously creating a whole new generation of epic antics for an entire new generation of laughing, cheering audiences, the first of which, *Chariots of Fur* starring Wile E. Coyote and the Road Runner, will be unleashed at about the same time as this book, Christmas 1994.

To so many, the work of Chuck Jones has prompted some of the most robust laughs of our lives. However, working *with* Chuck Jones, through *Bugs Bunny on Broadway, The Magical World of Chuck Jones, Chariots of Fur*, and now, *Peter and the Wolf*, has been the dream of a lifetime for me.

Aside from his brilliance as an artist, auteur, director, and everything else that this man does so uniquely and so brilliantly, Chuck Jones has been—and continues to be—my dear friend (and sometimes co-conspirator) and a mentor who has taught me so very much, not only about the fine art of storytelling in all its many guises, but even more so, about the joys of savoring life to the maximum . . . a life which, at the age of 82, Chuck Jones is living in a way that would leave most 25-year-olds panting for breath from sheer exhaustion.

So, it goes without saying that I send my eternal thanks to Chuck for allowing me the amazing privilege of working with him, side by side, on this *Peter and the Wolf*.

My deepest appreciation also goes to Terry Hershey, Craig Moody, and Mike Guttentag at Time-Warner Interactive, whose immediate and enthusiastic support served as the catalyst that first brought this project to life; to Larry Kirshbaum at Warner Books, for his unflagging belief in *Peter and the Wolf*; and to Lori Weintraub, at TW Kids, for making these wonderful characters accessible to a great many more children through her Read-Along series.

I also must thank the incredible Liney Li, who is tops on my list for sainthood, for designing this book—so beautifully—in such a short amount of time; much gratitude to our editor Nanscy Neiman; and love to our dear friend Linda Jones, who brought so much to the production.

This project would never have seen the light of day if it weren't for the steadfast inner circle of creative spirits who have dedicated the last eight months of their lives to the excellence of *Peter and the Wolf*.

First, and foremost, my thanks go to our talented and dedicated Co-executive Producer David Wong, who has led the forces so admirably, held all the pieces together, and conceived so many great ideas for the production; to our wonderful producer Jennifer Martin, who first brought us to Time-Warner Interactive, and who led us heroically through the maze of new technology surrounding this project; to the amazing Jackie Bees, who frequently juggled more balls at once than a circus veteran; and to our longtime partners Isabelle Zakin and Bruce Triplett (who also served as our able music supervisor). And, lastly, to my co-author, Janis Diamond, who so fantastically brought Peter's world to sparkling reality with a fresh imagination and a marvelous sense of childlike wonderment, I want to send much love and gratitude. Janis made the creative process of writing *Peter and the Wolf* an experience of sheer collaborative joy.

These are but six of the more than 150 artists, animators, designers, computer programmers, background painters, musicians, engineers, editors, and production associates who made this production a reality, and without whom there would now only be a blank page, an empty CD-ROM, or a lonely, unrecorded tape.

And to all those kids from the junior high school band who humored me and good-naturedly put up with *my* first *Peter and the Wolf*, way back in 1967—and to the good people of Pendleton who listened, and still managed to smile—thanks.

Finally, on a personal note, I want to sign off by voicing my heartfelt gratitude and appreciation to my first kindergarten teacher, Charlene Daugherty—who also happens to be my very patient and loving mother, and to whom I send all my love. And, I want to thank her for giving me—as she has given so many thousands of other children over the past four decades, and continues to do today—the gift of a lifetime . . . the love of music, art, and the magic of storytelling.

GEORGE DAUGHERTY
Los Angeles, 1994

FOREWORD

by Chuck Jones

It was George Daugherty who pointed out to me that the Coyote and Road Runner chase music was not a purloined theme from the Keystone Kops, but from an opera, no less: *The Bartered Bride* by Smetana. My tendency at that point was to retitle our new Road Runner cartoon *The Battered Bird*, which George would have thought wonderful, but the rest of the musically untutored world (including me) would have wondered about; a pun, I'm sorry to say, only works if you know the source of the word.

But imagine the cunning of Carl Stalling and Milt Franklin who, for over thirty years, composed and conducted all the wonderfully appropriate, wise, and yes downright funny musical accompaniment for *all* the nearly one thousand Warner Bros. animated cartoons, without telling us that they were sneakily introducing genuine classic music underlining these flippant little visual efforts of ours.

"Wagner's music is better than it sounds." So said Mark Twain, and I add, Warner's cartoon musical accompaniment is far more intricate, more musically sound, than it at first appears to be. Indeed, that accompaniment often saved what might have been a dull moment by a droll and unexpectedly joyous assault on the ear.

Now suddenly, to enhance and extend that tradition, another thirty years later, magically from under some musical toadstool, appears George Daugherty, *enfant terrible* and *enfant magnifique.*

All artists stand on pyramids, and the greatest of those know full well the fabric and structure of that pyramid and of the talent that has preceded them. No one knows this better than the brilliant George Daugherty. He is almost fifty years younger than I and at least fifty years musically wiser than he has any right to be.

But beyond that knowledge in George lurks the spark of lighthearted genius; the love of the absurd, the incongruous and the pixilated; plus the vital respect for his antecedents, necessary to greatness.

Because I have fallen uphill so often in my life, I suppose it should not surprise me that just when I find myself, at eighty-two, once again directing animated cartoons at Warner Bros., that George should drop into my life exactly at the moment he was uniquely needed, as well as the moment of my greatest need.

I should have known the first time I saw with wonder and delight George Daugherty conduct *Bugs Bunny on Broadway* that he was my kind of conductor. After all, anybody who wears cowboy boots with white tie and tails can't be all bad.

As it turned out, George is all good, or as near all good as an artist is safe to be. Yes, if Beethoven had been crossed with Hoagy Carmichael and a pixie, the result would have been something very close to George Daugherty.

I'm proud to happily work (?) with you again, George, as well as with the indomitable Peter and the irascible Wolf.

As Pogo would say, "It makes you humble and sort of proud."

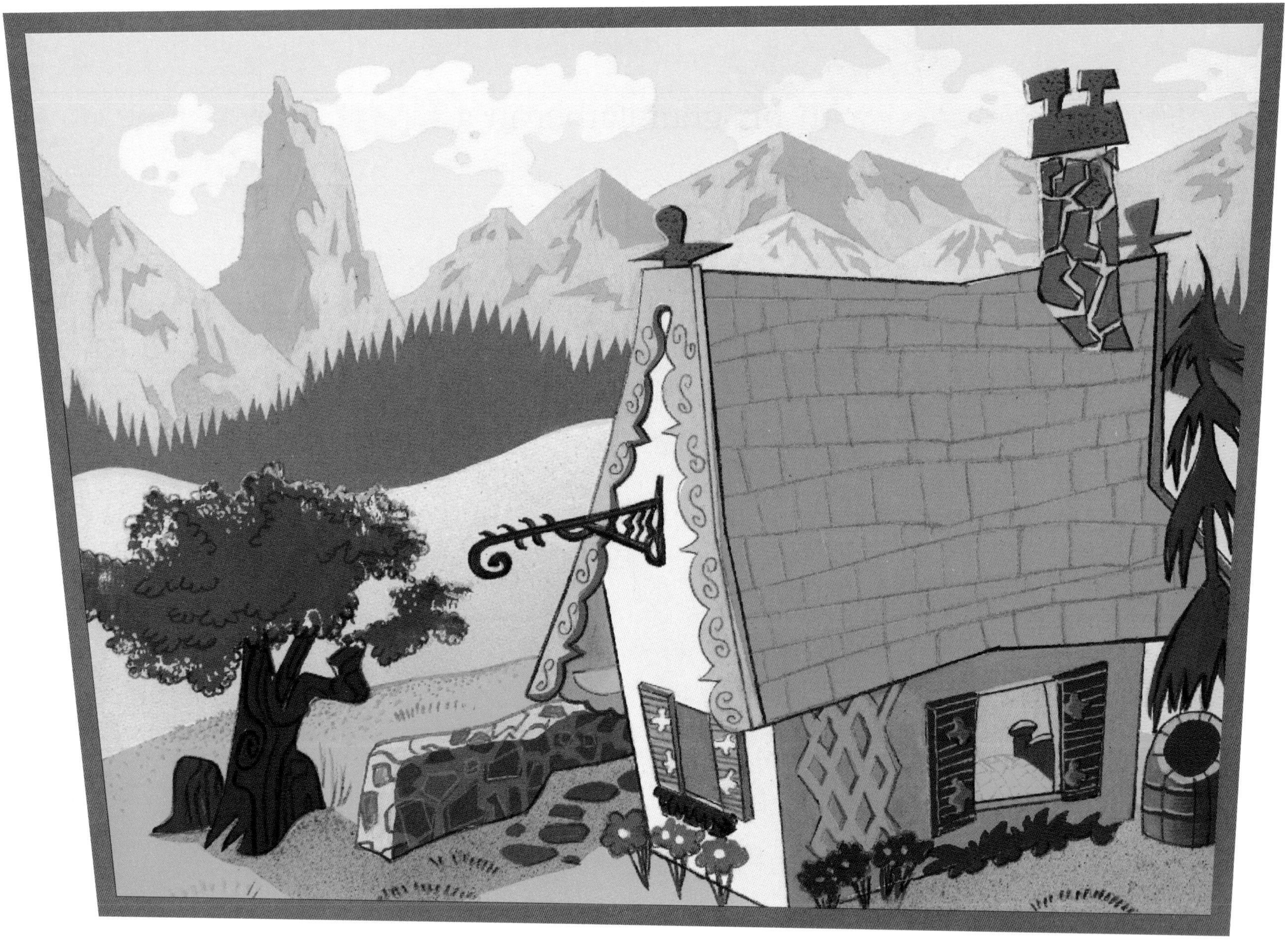

Peter lived with his grandfather in a quaint little cottage. Although tiny, it was warm and cozy, and made a wonderful home for the two of them.

The cottage had a blue shingled roof topped off by a stone chimney, and was surrounded by a stone wall with a gigantic rustic wooden gate. One large branch of a huge tree gently swooped over the wall.

Inside, there were only two rooms—the smallest of which Grandfather had recently turned into Peter's very own room. (After all, Peter was a big boy now, and big boys deserve their own room!)

Peter loved everything about his new room, especially the little window which gave him a bird's-eye view of the wonderful meadow that surrounded the cottage.

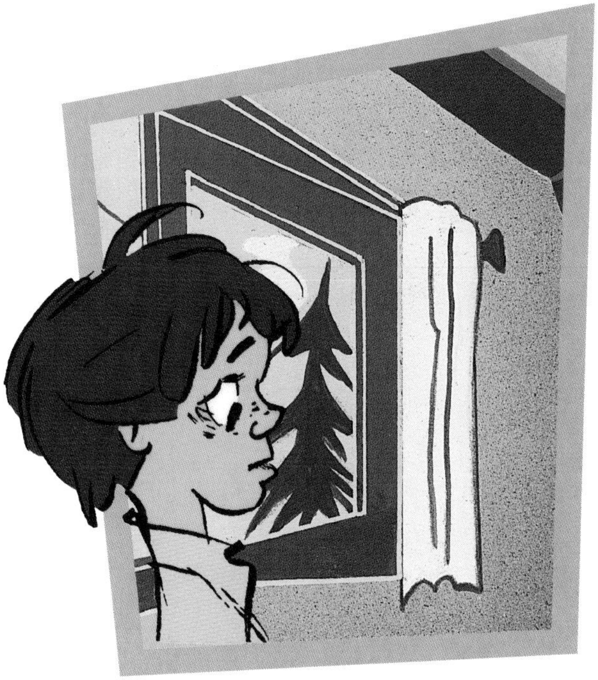

When Grandfather decided to give Peter his own room, he had this very window in mind. He thought that the boy and the meadow were growing up together, and he wanted Peter to see the magic of the four seasons . . . spring, summer, autumn, and winter . . . as they cycled through their miraculous changes every year.

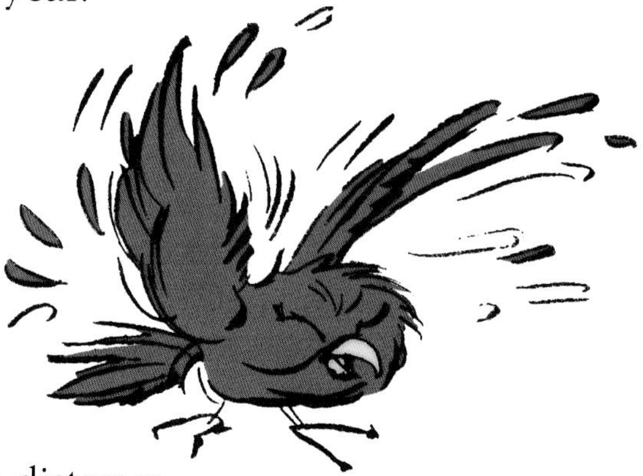

How clever Grandfather was, for now Peter could spend hours looking out at the beautiful meadow. Standing at his window, Peter could even see the majestic Matterhorn in the distance, soaring skyward to a snowy, icy cap at its crown.

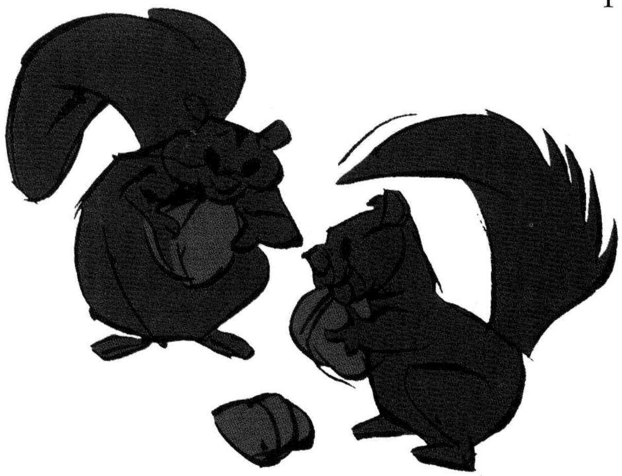

All about were lovely fields of green grass and tall, leafy trees bursting with the flurry of birds and the rustling of squirrels. In the center of the meadow stood a cool, blue pond, where lush flowers, tall grass, and willowy reeds caressed the water's edge.

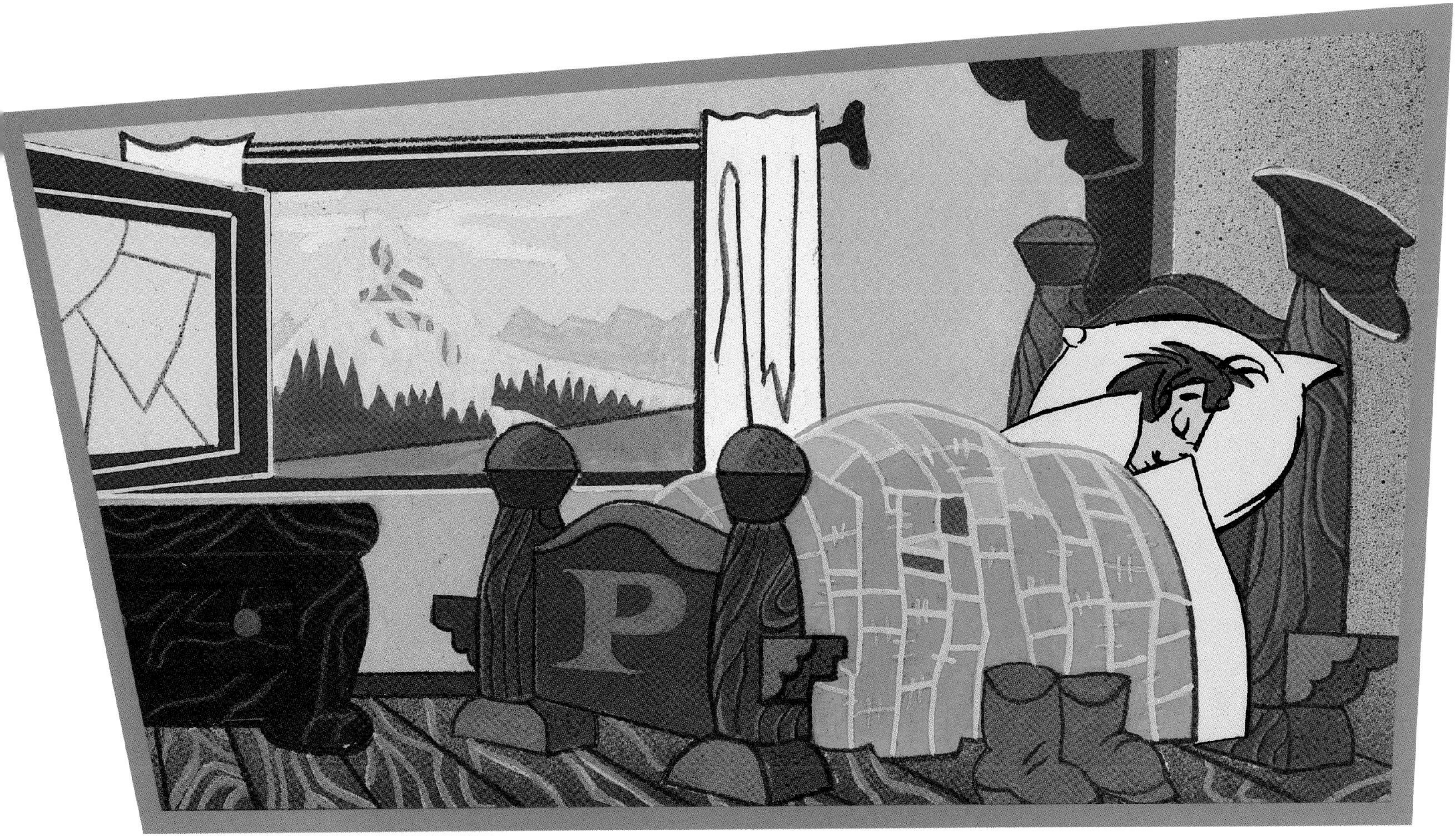

This was Peter's world, and a fantastic world it was.

Every night, he went to bed knowing that the sunrise of the next morning would bring him another chance to gaze out at his special kingdom—the meadow.

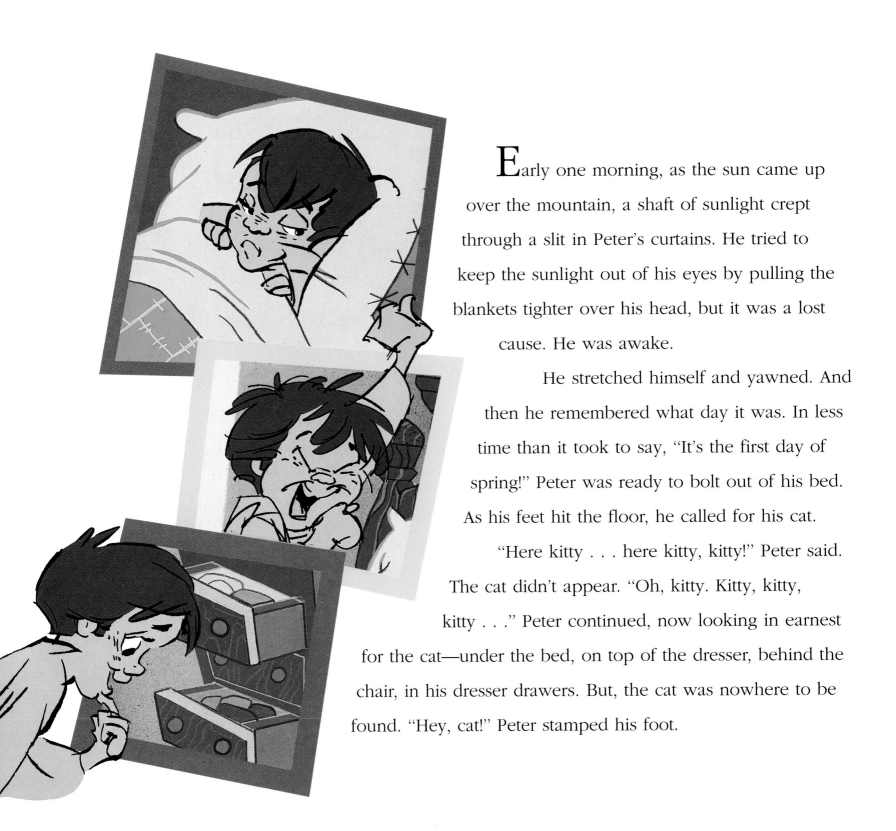

Early one morning, as the sun came up over the mountain, a shaft of sunlight crept through a slit in Peter's curtains. He tried to keep the sunlight out of his eyes by pulling the blankets tighter over his head, but it was a lost cause. He was awake.

He stretched himself and yawned. And then he remembered what day it was. In less time than it took to say, "It's the first day of spring!" Peter was ready to bolt out of his bed. As his feet hit the floor, he called for his cat.

"Here kitty . . . here kitty, kitty!" Peter said. The cat didn't appear. "Oh, kitty. Kitty, kitty, kitty . . ." Peter continued, now looking in earnest for the cat—under the bed, on top of the dresser, behind the chair, in his dresser drawers. But, the cat was nowhere to be found. "Hey, cat!" Peter stamped his foot.

"Where can that cat be?"

Peter wondered as he continued his search, this time looking under the tangled web of sheets and blankets. Peter tried whistling for the cat, but all that came out was a showery rush of sputtering air. Apparently, Peter hadn't learned to whistle, yet.

Now every child wants to whistle, and Peter was no exception. But whistling, like any other skill, is achieved only after lots of practice. So, as often happens, Peter got distracted while trying to whistle. He forgot all about his cat.

Walking around his room, Peter tried and tried and tried to whistle. He puckered his lips, he scrunched his lips. He blew his breath out, this way and that. But no whistle, only air.

Drawn over to the window by the sliver of sunlight, Peter kept trying. Nothing but more sputtering air!

Peter reached for the curtains to pull them. Suddenly, the breathtaking meadow was in front of him. A smile beamed across his freckled face. And before you knew it, an honest-to-goodness whistle came rolling out from between his puckered little lips. And what a whistle it was! It was a wonderful, musical tune.

Peter pulled his hand down enthusiastically as he let out a victorious cheer.

He opened the window and took a deep breath, and the fantastic smell of new flowers and fresh, young grass filled the air. Now he was sure that today was the very first day of spring . . . just like Grandfather had told him it would be.

The radiant, yellow morning sunshine streamed through the window, painting Peter in a golden glow. His eyes sparkled in delight as he yanked his clothes from the drawers and quickly started getting dressed, still whistling all the way.

After all, it had been a long, cold winter and the warm sun and fresh cool breeze were exactly what Peter needed. In fact, Peter decided that what he *really* needed was a walk in the meadow.

Of course, there was only one little problem . . . Grandfather. As much as Grandfather loved the beauty of the meadow, *he* knew that there were dangerous animals lurking just on the other side of the glen, at the forest's edge.

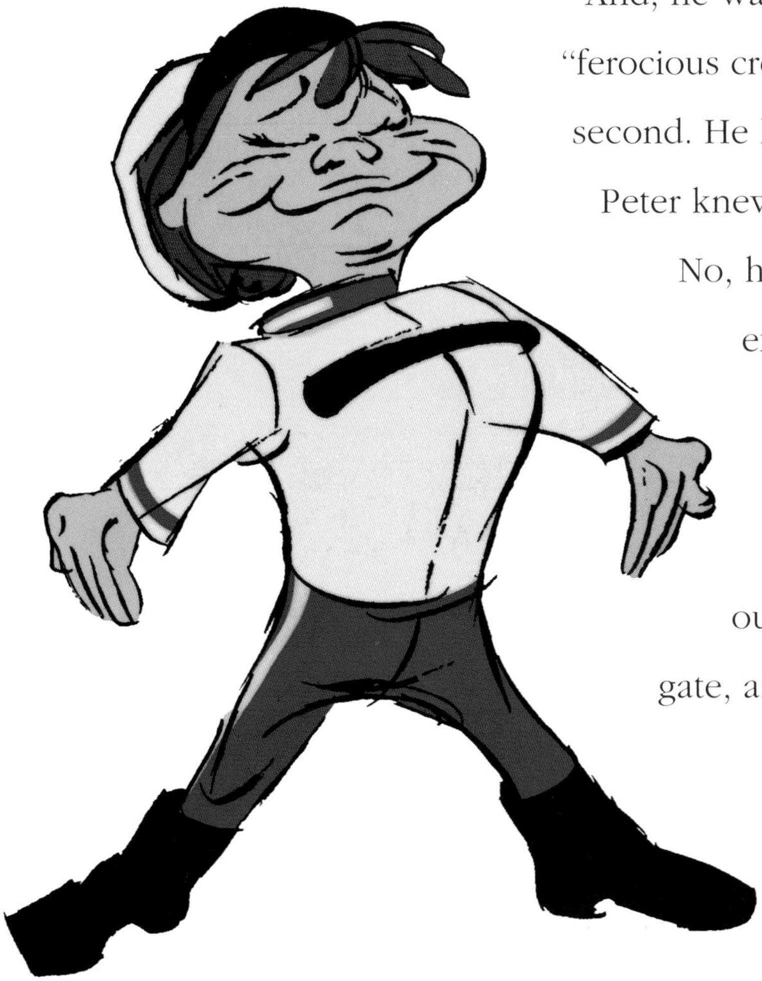

And, he was always warning Peter about wolves and other "ferocious creatures." But Peter didn't believe him for a second. He loved his grandfather with all his heart, but Peter knew he was just being an old fuddy-dud.

No, he was sure of it. A walk in the meadow was exactly what the first day of spring called for.

So making sure he wasn't seen by Grandfather, Peter (who now looked quite dapper in his military school uniform) sneaked out of the house, quietly opened the big garden gate, and walked out into the meadow.

His meadow.

With eyes bright with awe and delight, he walked through glorious banks of flowers, still glistening with the morning dew as they opened their petals to the shimmering light. The clear morning sunlight glistened off the rippling waters of the cool, blue pond.

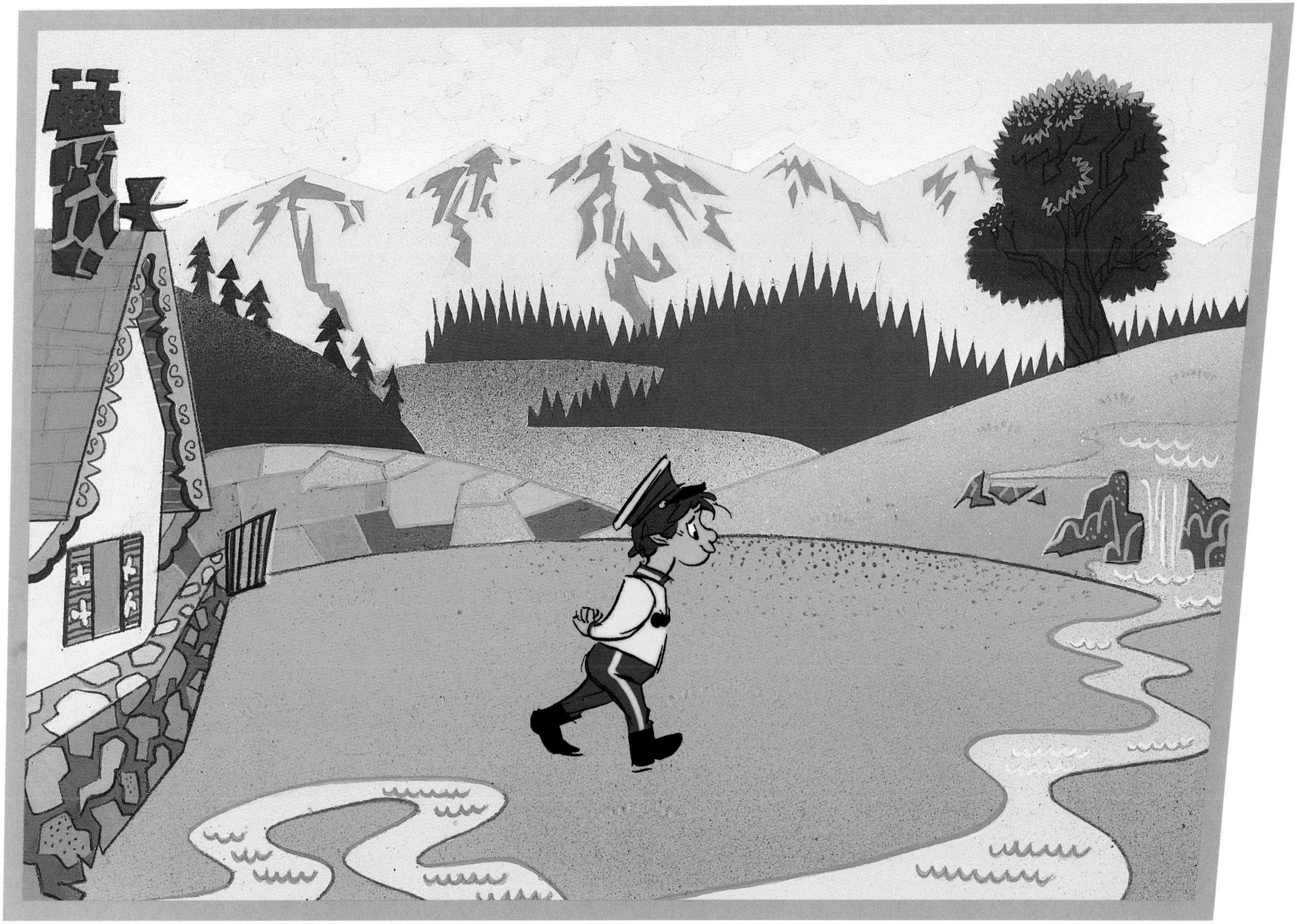

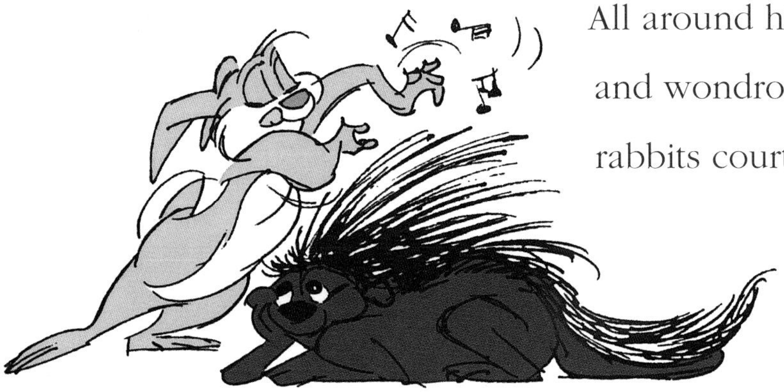

All around him, the meadow was teeming with the new life and wondrous fresh smells of spring; porcupines played, rabbits courted, and a mother squirrel scampered with her babies. Two deer taught their fawn to hunt for berries, and a lone ladybug sunbathed on a dewy morning glory petal. A fantastic waterfall, fed by the Matterhorn's icy stream, emptied her waters into the pond and watched over the entire scene like a proud mother.

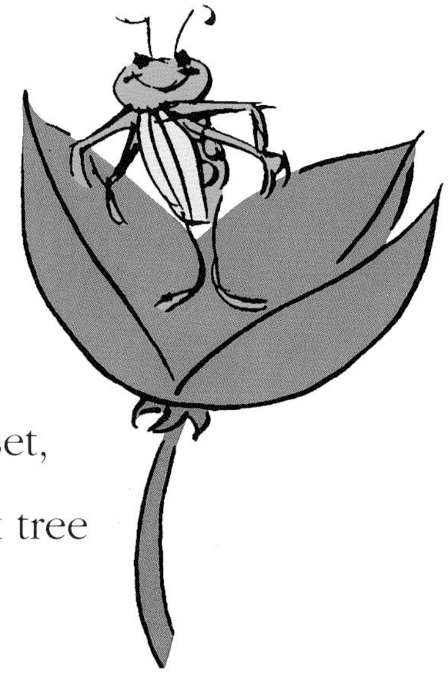

In the distance, Peter spotted his favorite climbing tree. He decided climbing was the perfect pastime for the perfect spring day. His course set, Peter set out for the big oak tree on the pond's bank.

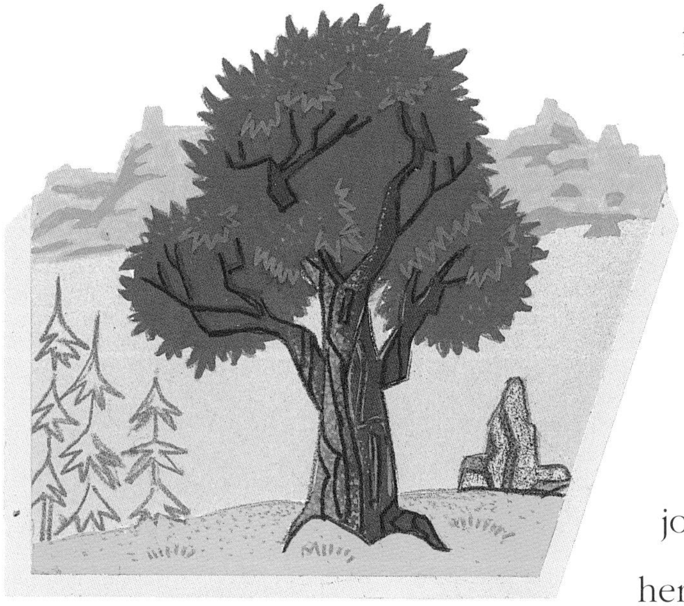

• • •

Suddenly, a bird darted down from the tree and joyously circled Peter's head. The cheerful chirps of her flutey voice greeted Peter like a joyful song.

"Hey, I'm glad to see you, too!" Peter laughed as the bird zoomed around him.

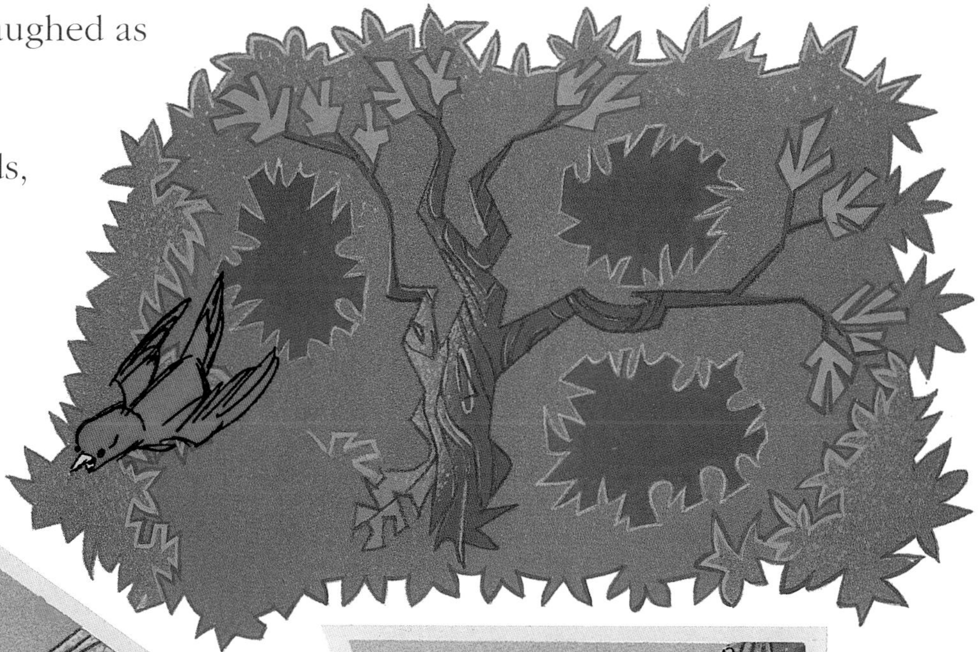

Peter and the bird were old friends, and he listened in wide-eyed wonder when she told him she had something to show him. Then she darted off toward the big oak tree. Periodically, she would hover in midair, turning back toward Peter to make sure that he was following her. He was.

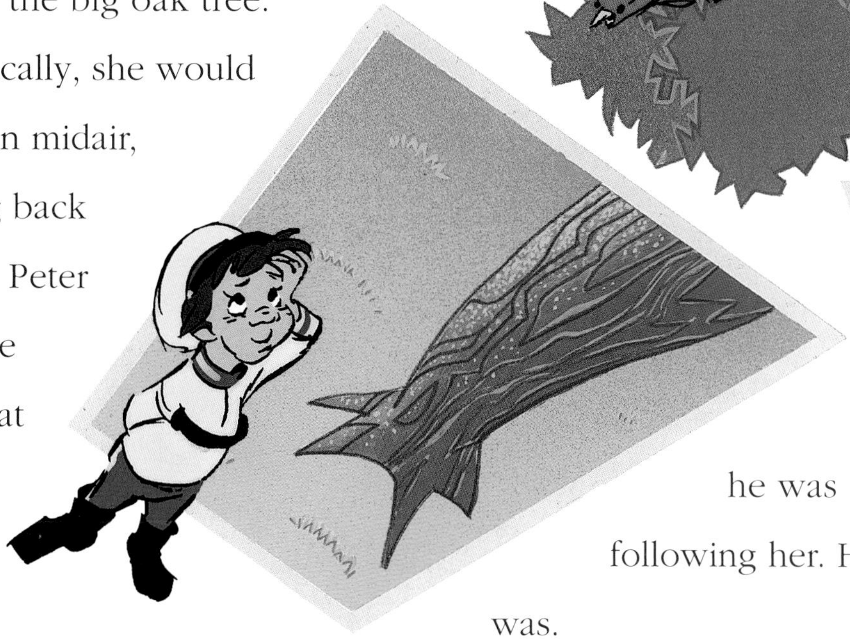

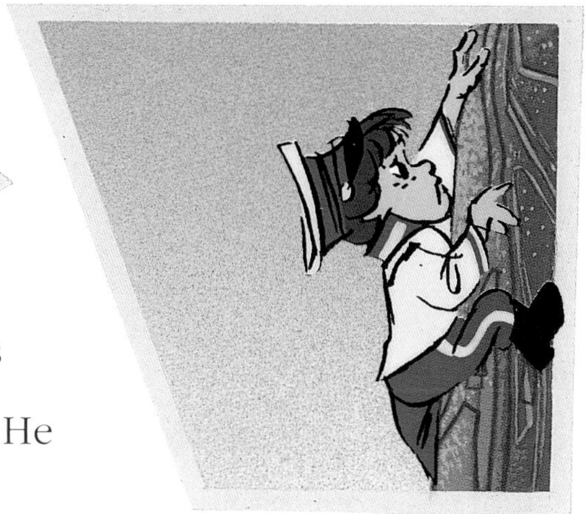

They came to the tree, and Peter started climbing, doing his best to keep up with the bird. After all, the bird could fly, and Peter had to climb. But Peter happened to be a terrific tree climber, and finally, they reached a large branch at the very top. Peter was panting, and starting to get a little impatient.

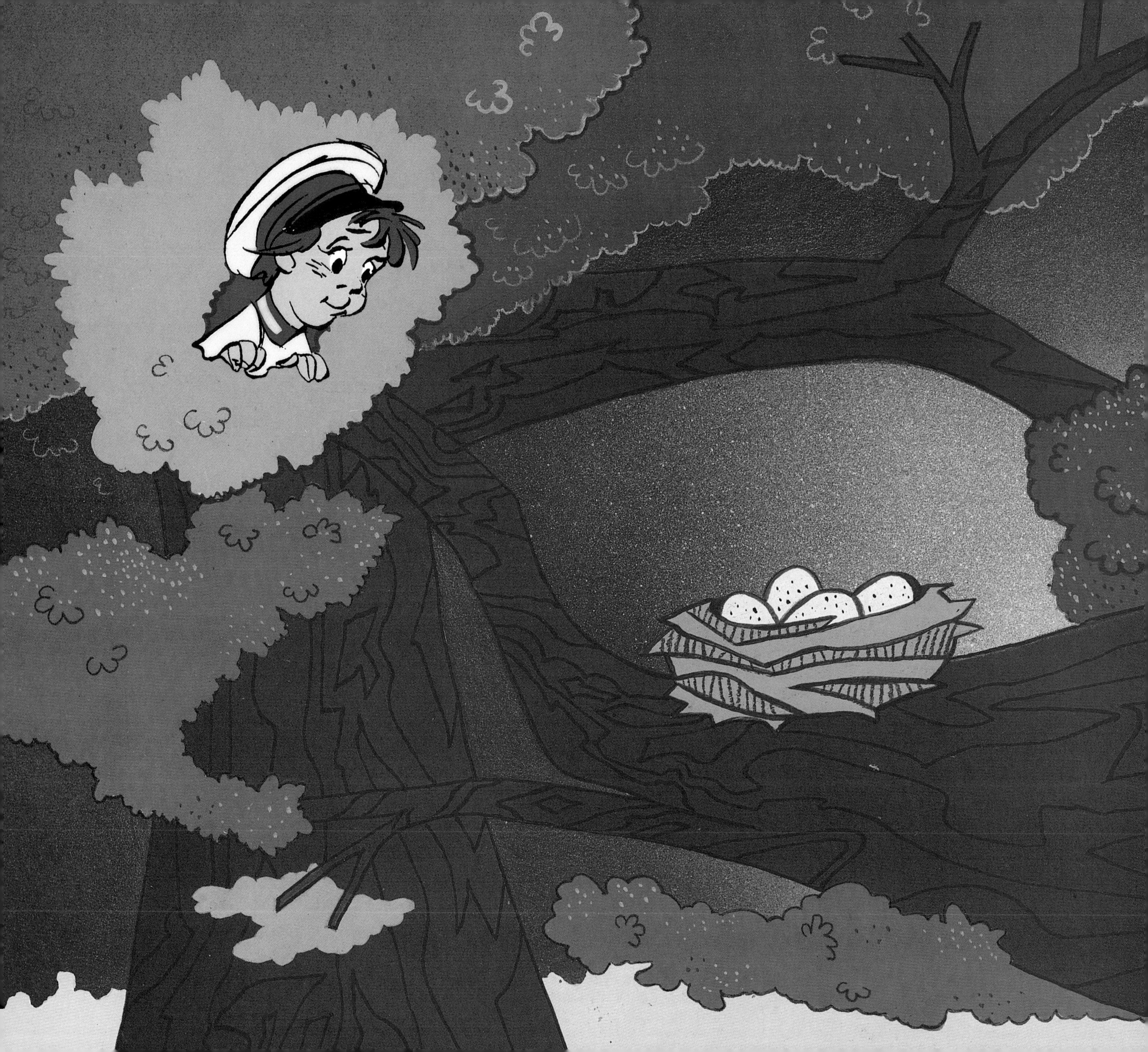

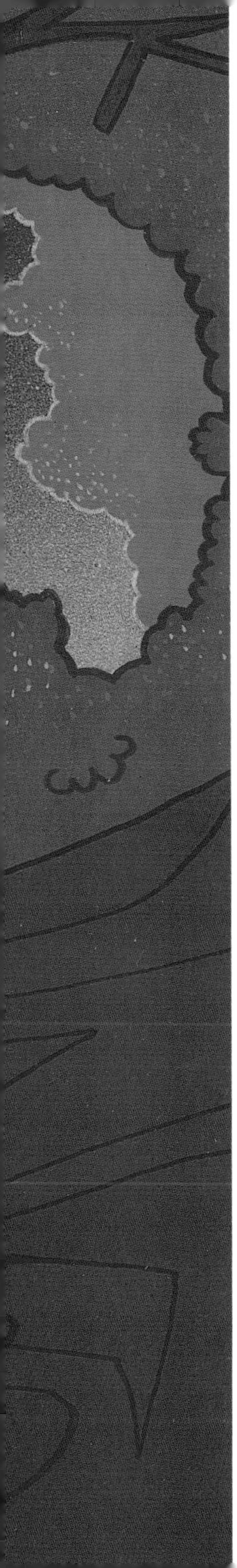

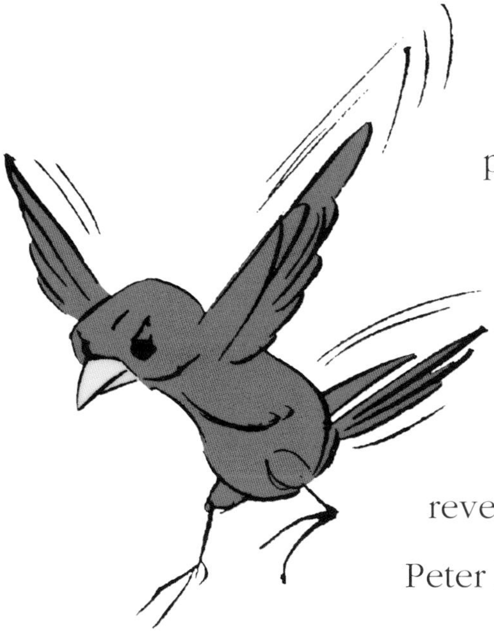

"So what *is* it?" he asked the bird, who was poking her head out through the leaves. Before she could answer, though, Peter saw something.

"Oh-h-h-h-h-h!!" was all Peter could utter, for he held his breath now, in suspense. He silently watched the bird proudly clear away the leaves, revealing a cozy nest filled with six recently laid eggs. Peter leaned forward for a closer look. He saw that the eggs were a brilliant blue with black spots. Of course, Peter immediately tried to pick one up.

"You can look, but you can't touch," the bird warned Peter, with a hyperflutter of her wings.

But Peter didn't take "no" lightly and climbed to a higher branch. Utterly fearless, he hung upside down, trying to touch the eggs when the bird was not looking.

But she *was* looking, and the bird twittered around Peter's head until he backed away.

So, Peter dropped down onto another branch and walked across it like a tightrope, edging closer to the nest—only to be shooed away by the bird again. And again. And again.

"Oh brother!" he sighed. Annoyed and frustrated, he flopped right back down onto the branch where the nest was perched. As was the bird. Now she became even more nervous, for Peter's sudden movement had jarred her nest.

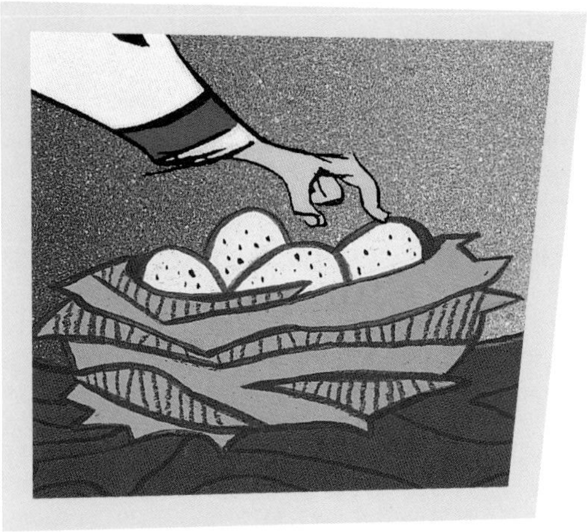

Peter sat quietly for a moment. Then he swung his legs back and forth, pretending he didn't give a hoot about the bird's nest. But he did smile at her. And she hopped closer to him.

The bird cocked her head, considering. "Well, maybe if you're quiet, you can touch them," she seemed to say with another flutter of her wings.

"I promise!" Peter eagerly replied.

So, very, very carefully, Peter reached out and touched one of the sky-blue eggs with the very tip of his finger.

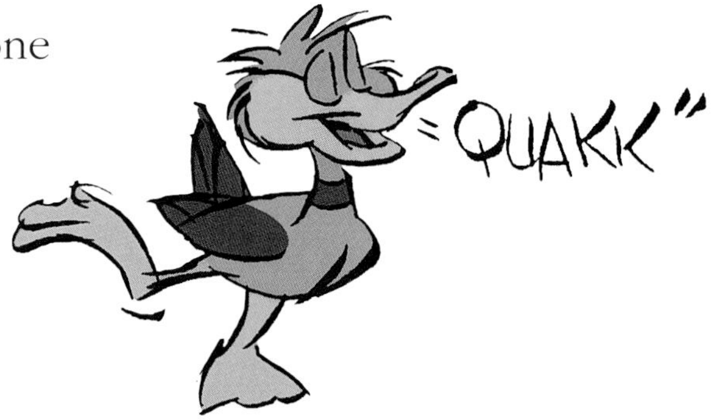
"QUAKK"

• • •

Just then, a fluffy, fat duck, contentedly quacking to himself like a reedy old oboe, began his trek from the house to the pond, waddling all the way. The duck was very happy because Peter had forgotten to shut the gate. Now he could have a nice swim in the pond. It had been a long winter for him, too.

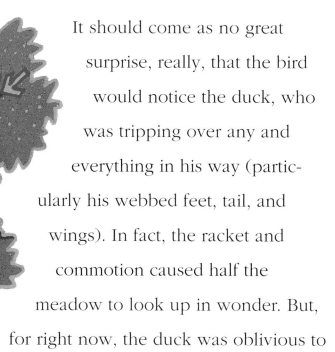

It should come as no great surprise, really, that the bird would notice the duck, who was tripping over any and everything in his way (particularly his webbed feet, tail, and wings). In fact, the racket and commotion caused half the meadow to look up in wonder. But, for right now, the duck was oblivious to all else and continued his ridiculous journey to the pond.

The bird ruffled her feathers when Peter noticed the duck, too. She definitely didn't like having to share Peter with anyone else, especially this poor ornithological excuse. So she flew out of the tree and circled around the duck to get a closer look.

"How could any creature who has so much trouble getting from one place to another, and on the ground, no less, ever call itself a bird," she called to the duck, as she landed at his feet with a hop, hop, hop.

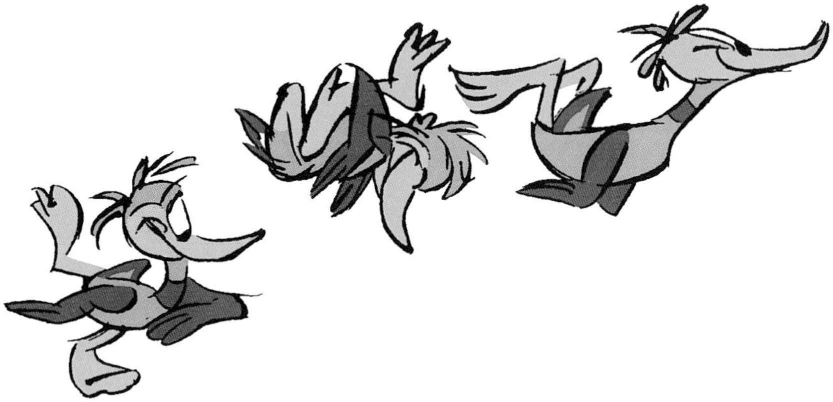

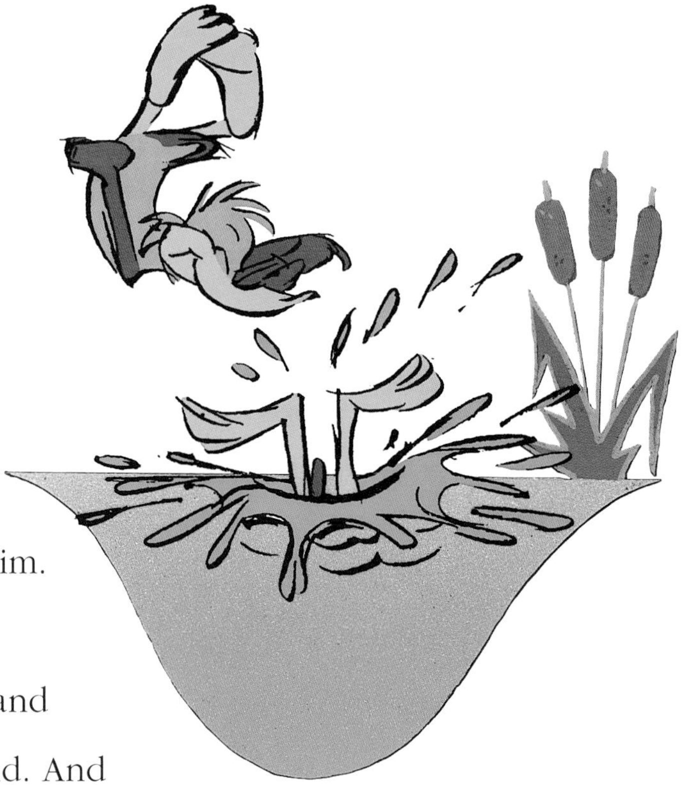

The duck, however, didn't even notice the bird. And why should he? He was on his way to a wonderful swim.

He clumsily slid down the bank, tripping and stumbling one last time over his orange webbed feet, and dizzily paused at the water's edge for just a split second. And then, with one last waddle of his fat, feathery body, he dove into the blue, clear water.

The poor bird couldn't contain herself and took to the air, once again circling the duck. But by now, the duck was in pond heaven, swimming wide leisurely circles, and a figure eight or two.

The bird, however, didn't like to be ignored. "How can you call yourself a bird down there in the water like that!" she yelled to the duck, hoping to catch his attention.

By now she was hopping around the pond's bank, making quite a racket and stirring up so much commotion that the entire meadow could hear her.

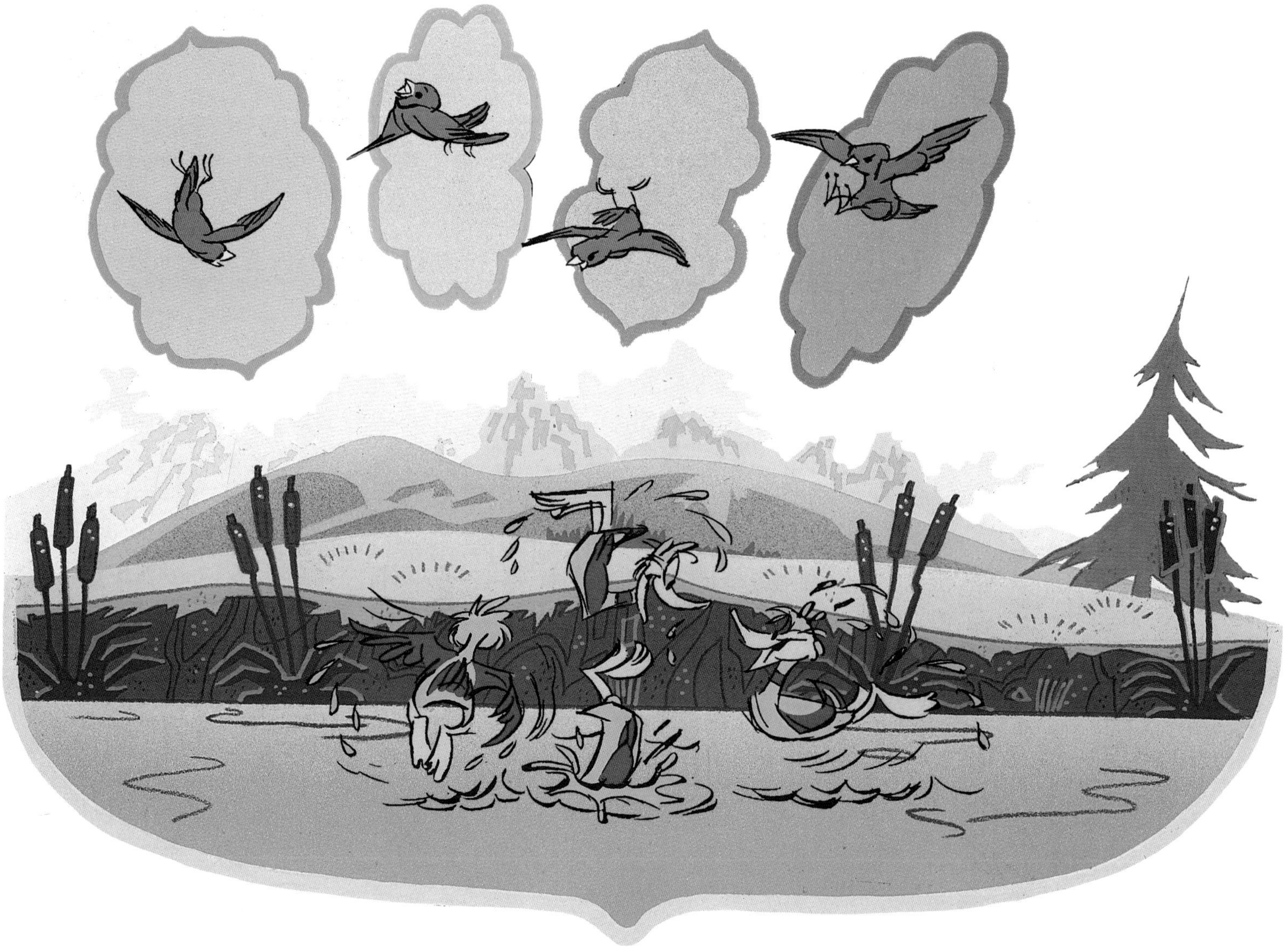

"Why no self-respecting bird can swim!" the bird yelled out louder to the duck.

No one, not the mother squirrel, the father deer, the teenage porcupine, or the cute courting rabbits, could believe the duck was still ignoring the bird. And they stopped whatever they were doing and gathered around the pond's bank to watch.

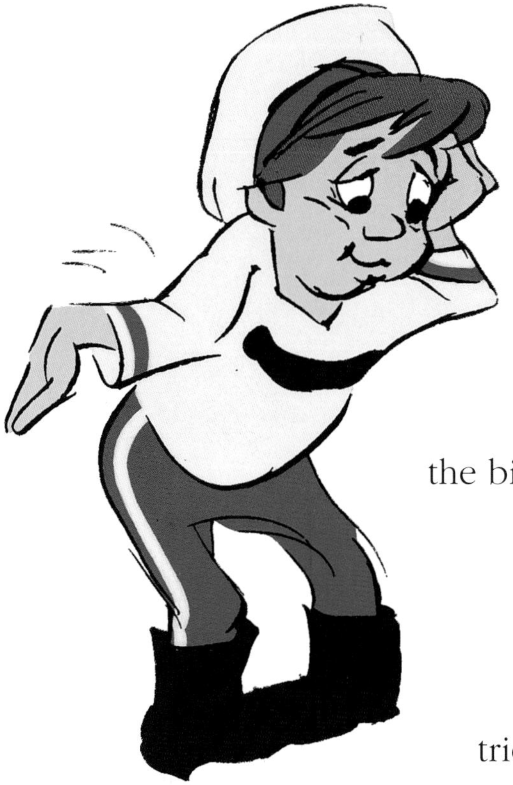

Even Peter scrambled down the tree and ran onto the pond's bank, joining in the melee. "Yeah, how come!" he said, momentarily taking the bird's side in this feathery argument. But still, the duck swam along doing his best to shut out the bird's shrill yapping.

"Listen to me! Get up here in the air, where a bird belongs!" the bird shouted as she buzzed around the duck's head.

"Get out of the pond, right now!" she continued adamantly.

"Yeah, right now!" chimed in Peter.

Well, all of this commotion did start to get to the duck. He tried his best to shut out the bird's tirade, but all of this did take its toll. The pace of his swimming began to quicken, and his nautical patterns started to get wild and reckless.

It certainly didn't help when the rest of the meadow's population joined the argument, shouting encouragement or disagreement, depending on whose side they had taken.

The noise was incredible. And it went on and on like that until suddenly, amidst all the confusion, Peter's cat appeared in the meadow.

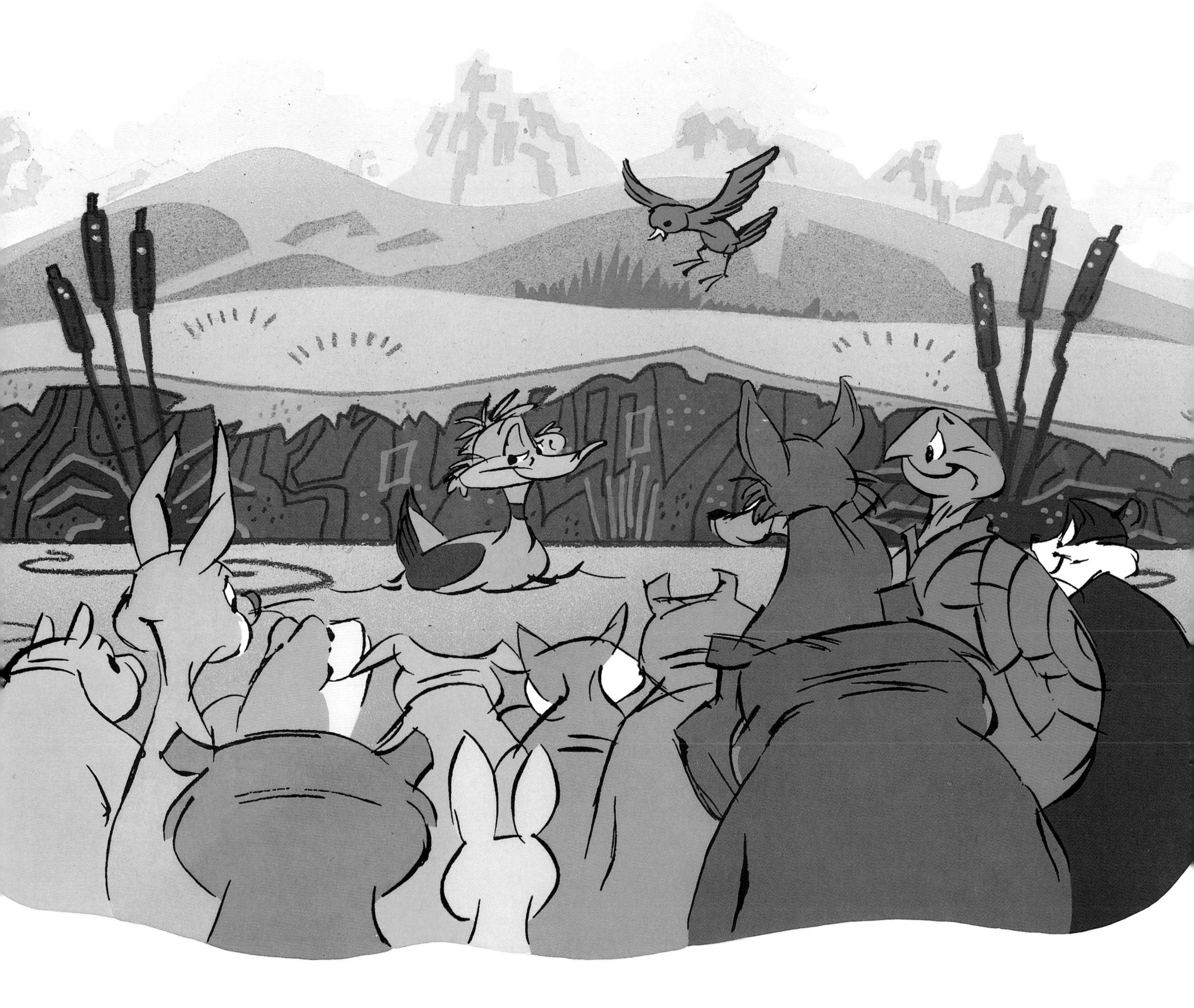

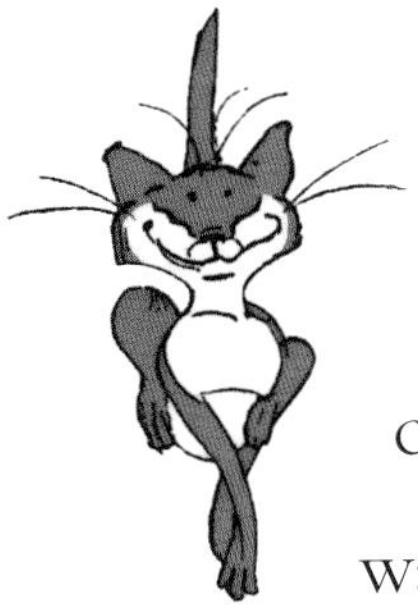

The cat, an independent and somewhat persnickety fellow, cast an imperious glance as he studied the meadow. All the while his tail was moving like a metronome, until he spotted the bird. Then his tail stopped in midbeat. Straight up.

"Hmmmm, the bird is busy arguing with the duck," the cat thought. "So I'll just get a little closer and maybe I can grab her. I could use a little breakfast."

His plan decided, the cat crept stealthily through the tall grass . . .

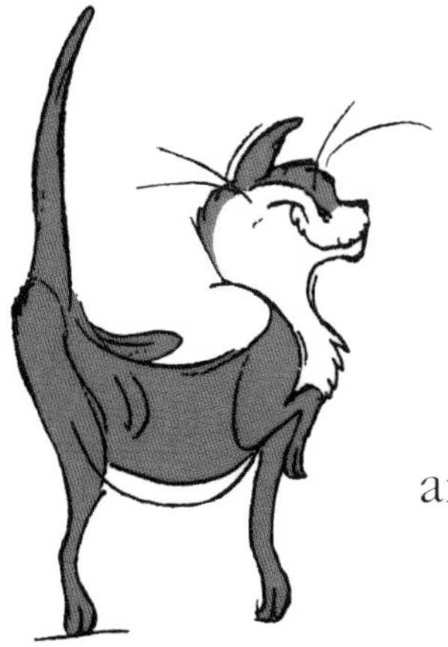

disappearing, reappearing, and
disappearing again, like
a chameleon,
hiding here
and there.

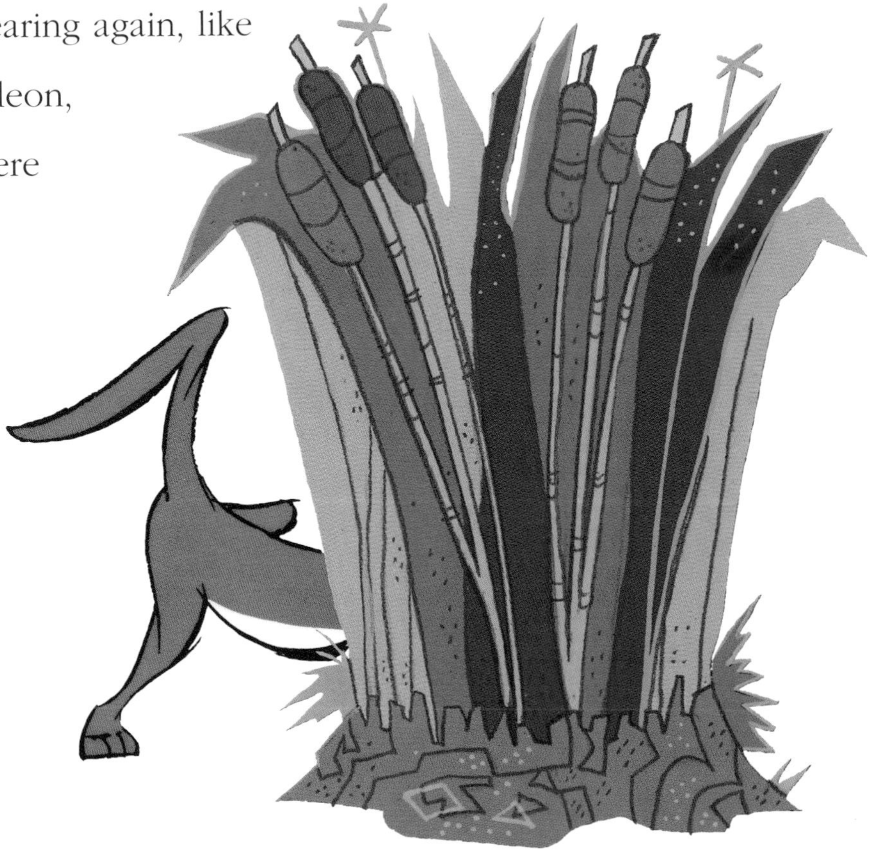

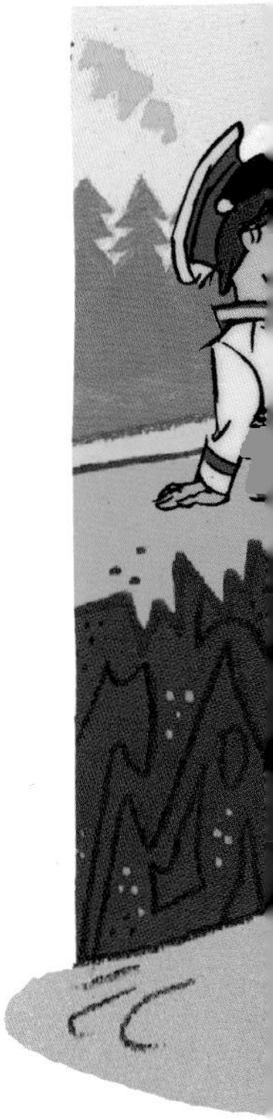

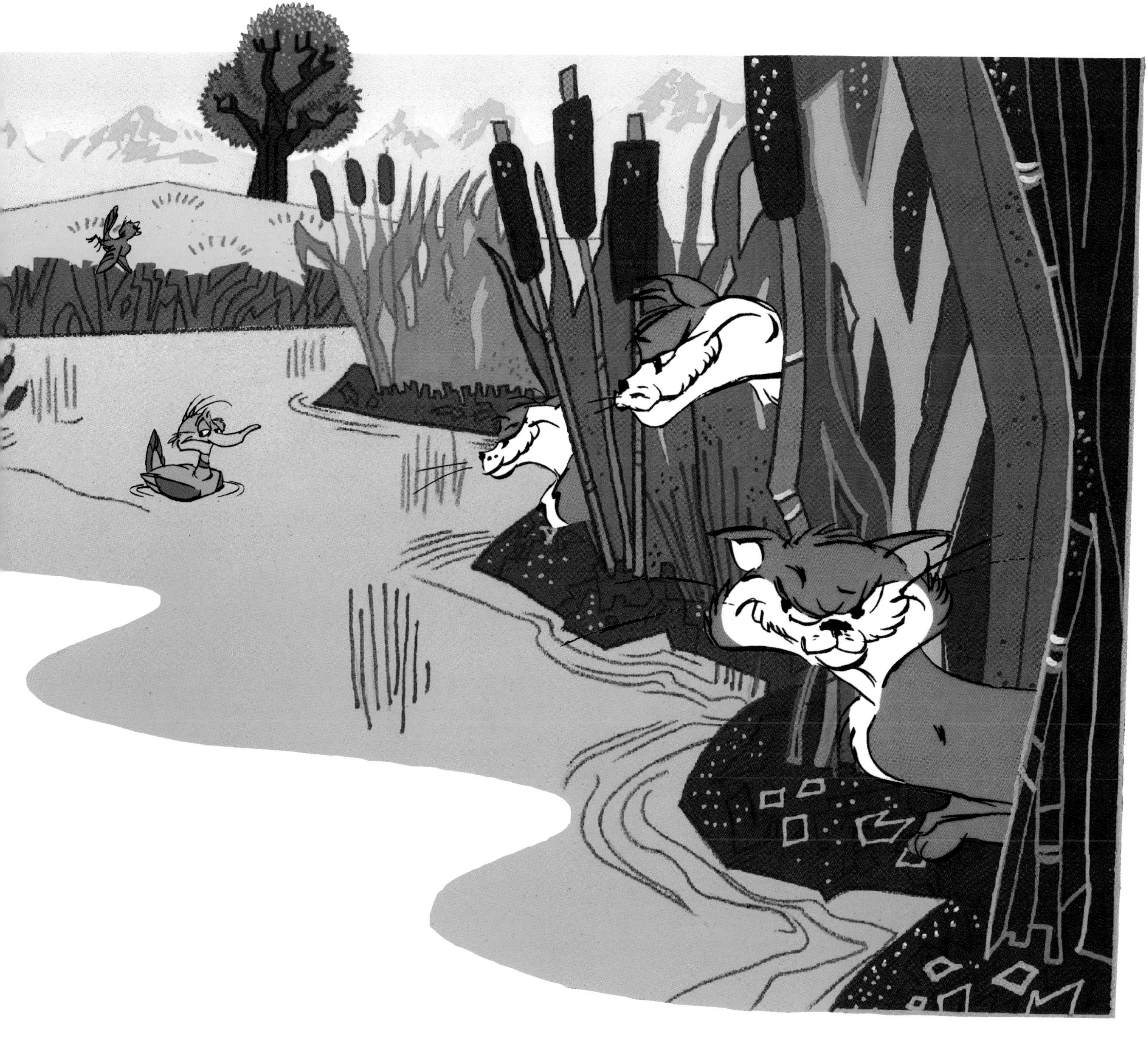

All the while, the bird was still hopping frantically around the pond, trying to engage the duck in some meaningful dialogue.

Instead, though, the duck got more and more flustered, splashing water all over the place. Indeed, not the intended result!

And in the middle of it all was Peter, joyously running back and forth amid all the commotion. This was definitely a great way to spend a morning, thought Peter. He was certainly getting a lot more excitement from his morning walk than he had expected.

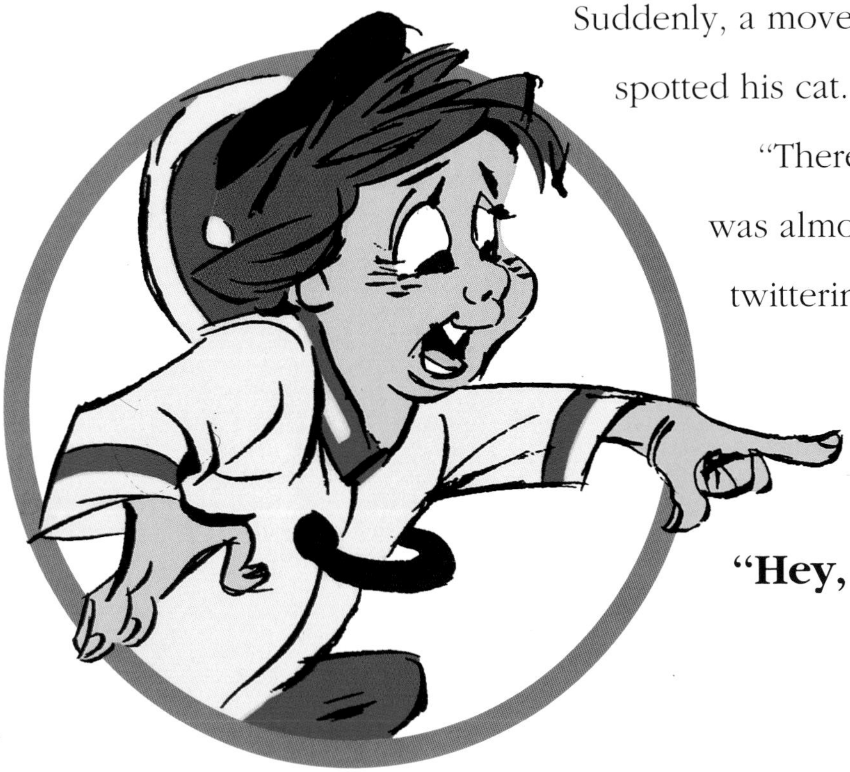

Suddenly, a movement in the grass caught his attention. He spotted his cat.

"There you are," Peter said to the cat. But, the cat was almost upon the bird, who was so busy twittering at the duck that she hadn't even noticed the feline attack being mounted behind her. Peter, however, saw what was about to happen.

"Hey, look out!" Peter warned the bird.

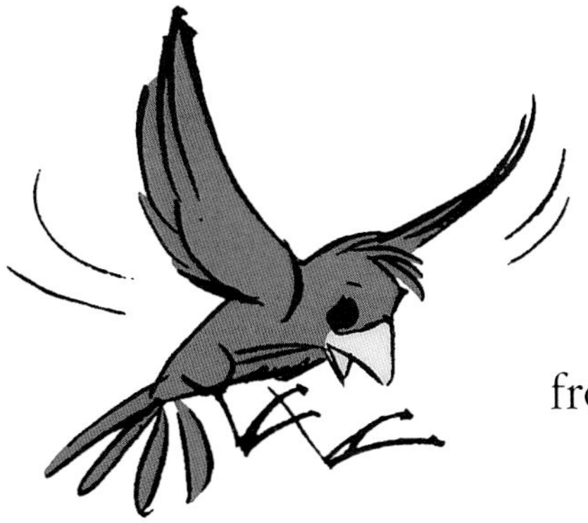

In a flurry, the bird took to the air, flying quickly away from the leaping cat.

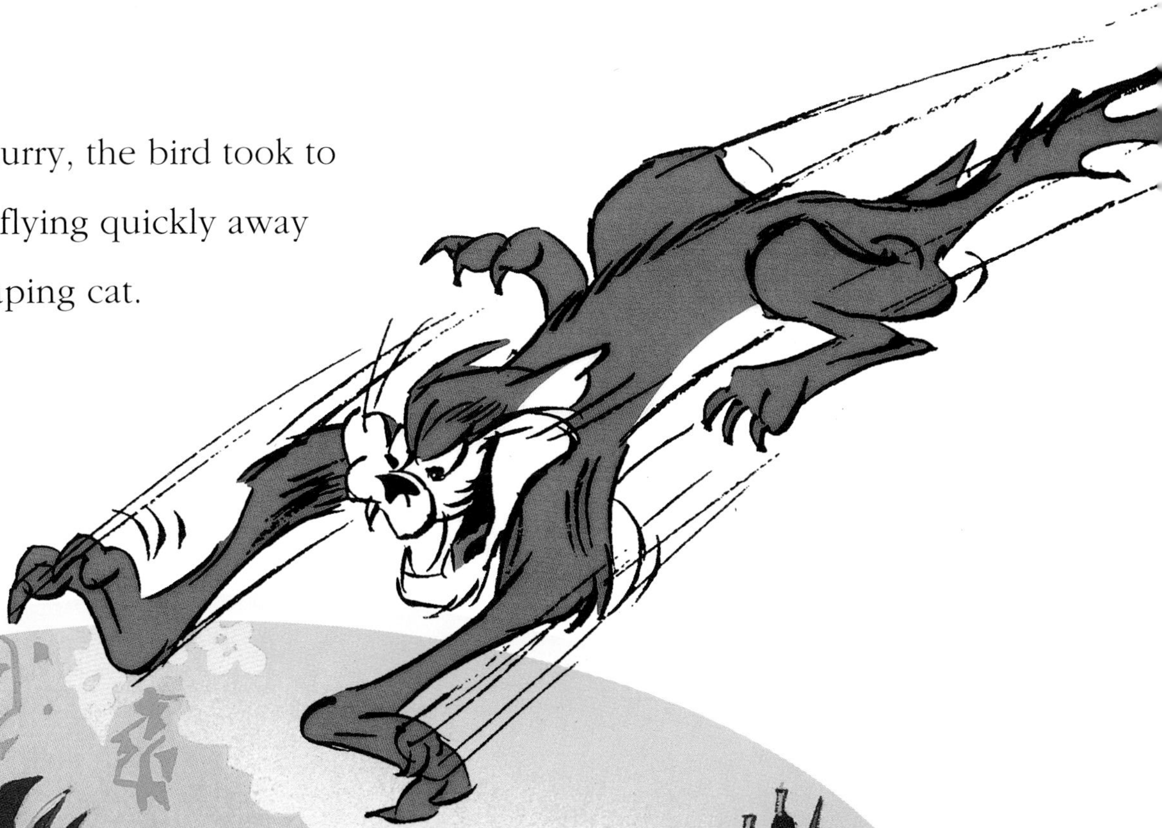

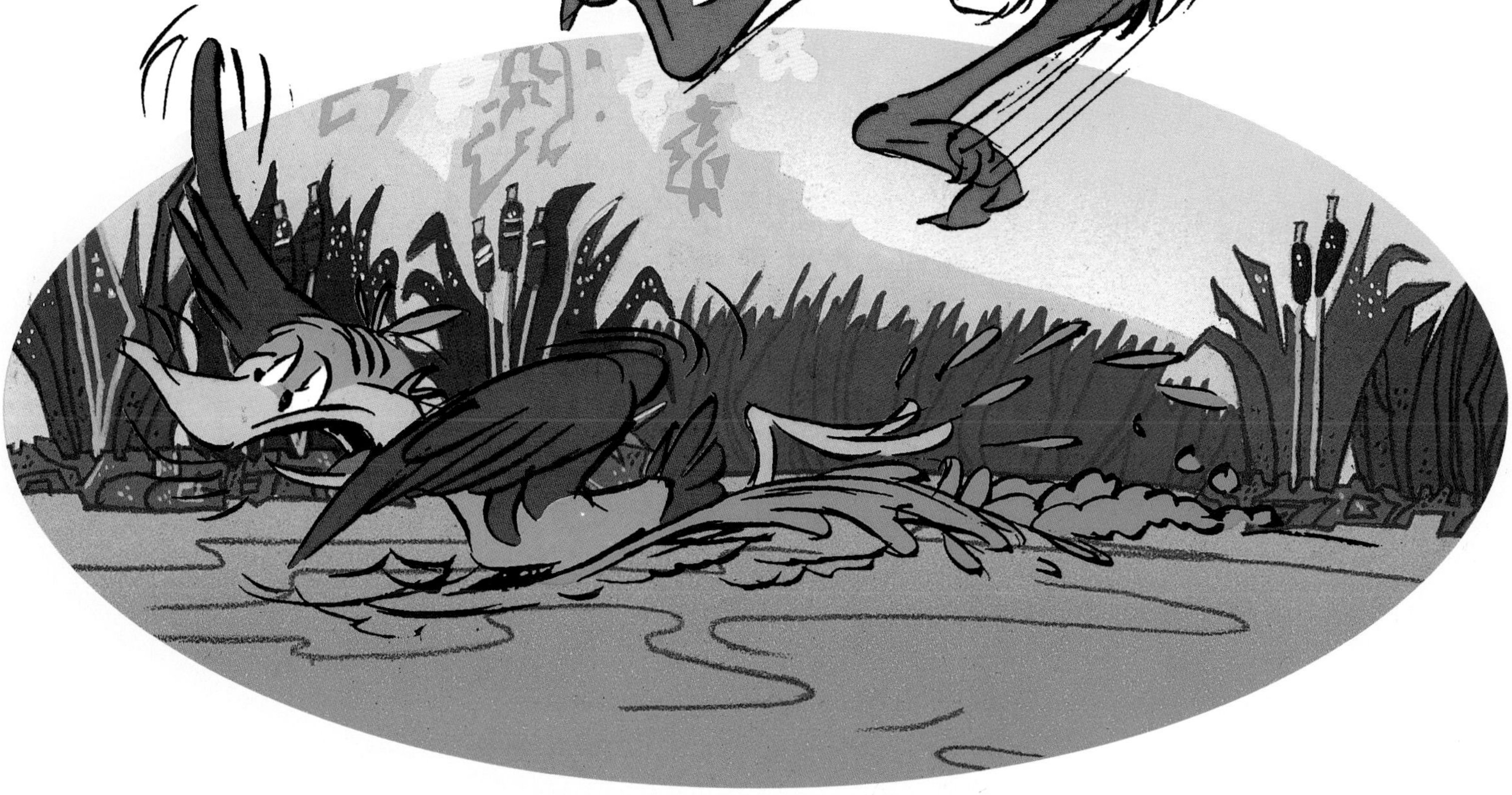

In no time at all, she was settled back safe in the tree right next to her nest of eggs.

The cat, in the meantime, had overshot *his* leap, and found himself in the shallow water at the pond's edge. It was not a great place for a cat.

Meanwhile, the duck was becoming more and more frazzled (who could blame him?!) and he zoomed back to the middle of the pond, swimming frantically in a circle. "Quack, quack, quack!"

The cat ignored the quibbly-quabbly duck. Instead, he quickly shook himself off, tried to put the watery cat-astrophy behind him, and made a beeline for the oak tree.

You see, the cat had spotted
the bird way up in the tree,
and was deliberately watching
her every move out of the corner
of his eye. And then, just like that,
he decided that all of this was truly
too much trouble for such a small
snack. By the time he climbed way up
to the top of the tree, figured the cat, the
bird would have flown away, anyhow.

Of course, the cat could swim out to the middle of the
pond, if he wanted to. But, a respectable cat would never *swim*. No, not even for a nice plump
duck. A cat, after all, did have his self-respect and personal image to think about.

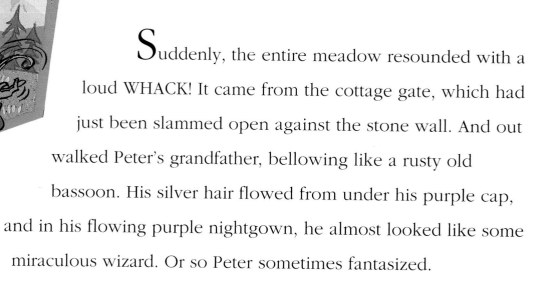

Suddenly, the entire meadow resounded with a loud WHACK! It came from the cottage gate, which had just been slammed open against the stone wall. And out walked Peter's grandfather, bellowing like a rusty old bassoon. His silver hair flowed from under his purple cap, and in his flowing purple nightgown, he almost looked like some miraculous wizard. Or so Peter sometimes fantasized.

At any rate, Grandfather wasted no time as he quickly hobbled toward Peter.

"Peter? Peter! What are you doing out there in the meadow, Peter!" the spry old man yelled after his grandson. Although Grandfather looked stern and solemn, his eyes twinkled merrily on either side of his funny nose.

"Young man, if I've told you once, I've told you a million times, this meadow is a DANGEROUS PLACE, a very, very, dangerous place!" he bellowed some more. But Peter pretended he didn't hear him.

"The edge of the forest is right over there, you know that! And there are all kinds of ferocious creatures living behind those trees. Why, what if a wolf came out of the forest all of a sudden? What if he gobbled you up? Where would you be then?" Grandfather continued.

"You'd be in his belly, that's where you'd be! I'm telling you, Peter, once and for all, this meadow is no place for boys to just play around in without a care in the world," Grandfather continued with a firm yank on the young boy's sleeve. Then he started leading Peter home.

Naturally, Peter didn't want to go home. He was having too good a time in the meadow. And he certainly wasn't listening to Grandfather. No, instead, at the mention of wolves Peter's eyes glazed over. He started to daydream.

And it was quite a daydream, all about wolves and Peter, who found himself deep in the dark and gloomy forest. He was stalking what appeared to be a pack of gigantic wolves. Now, ordinarily, you'd expect a boy to be frightened, but that's what was so wonderful about this daydream. Peter was anything but frightened. Boys like Peter are not afraid of wolves!

"Yeah, boys like me are not afraid of wolves," Peter declared, whipping out a rope. (In his dream, that is!) And Peter triumphantly lassoed the wolves, all at once. He laughed a victorious laugh.

"Me afraid of stupid old wolves? Absolutely not, no way, not in a million years. Bring on the rest of the wolves . . ."

"Peter! Who are you talking to?"

The sharp edge of Grandfather's voice rudely interrupted Peter's otherwise perfect daydream. And Peter was quickly jolted back to reality.

"I said, who are you talking to?"

Peter laughed a nervous laugh.

"A wolf is nothing to laugh about! It's serious business. Very serious business!" said Grandfather.

"Oh brother," said Peter under his breath.

"Are you making fun of me?" roared Grandfather.

"No," answered Peter, very, very quietly.

"I'd think *not*," Grandfather grumbled as he grabbed Peter by the shoulder and continued walking him back toward the gate and the cottage.

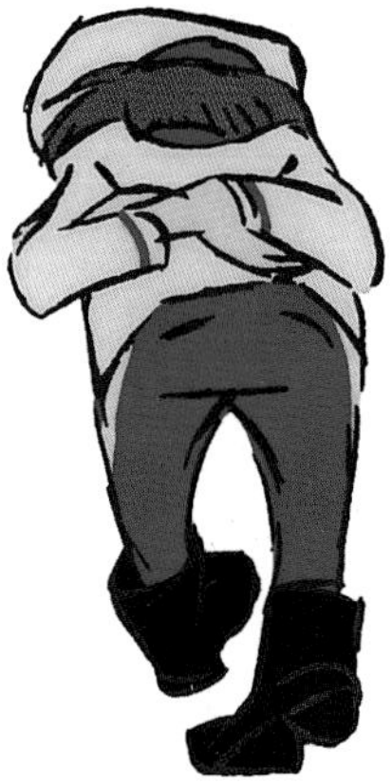

"C'mon, boy. I've had enough of this. More than enough," Grandfather said. "I'm an old man now. I have more important things to do than to chase you around the meadow every day. You're a big boy now. You should know better! I certainly taught you better.

"Now young man, you get back into the house right now, before I . . . I . . ."

And before Grandfather had a chance to finish his sentence, the gate slammed shut. The meadow, at least for an instant, became blissfully peaceful again.

• • •

Well, no sooner had Peter gone, than a wolf did appear. A big, gray one. He walked boldly out of the forest and into the meadow, making no noise at all except for the foreboding rustle of the leaves and branches as they crackled under his feet.

He sniffed here. He sniffed there. And then, he sniffed the scent of duck. *The* duck.

With a sneer on his craggy face, he pulled himself up to his full, intimidating height, and sniffed the air once again. Yes, he definitely smelled duck, and to the wolf, fresh duck sounded like it would just hit the spot. His sneer got even bigger, and the sun sparkled off a sharp, glistening, gold tooth.

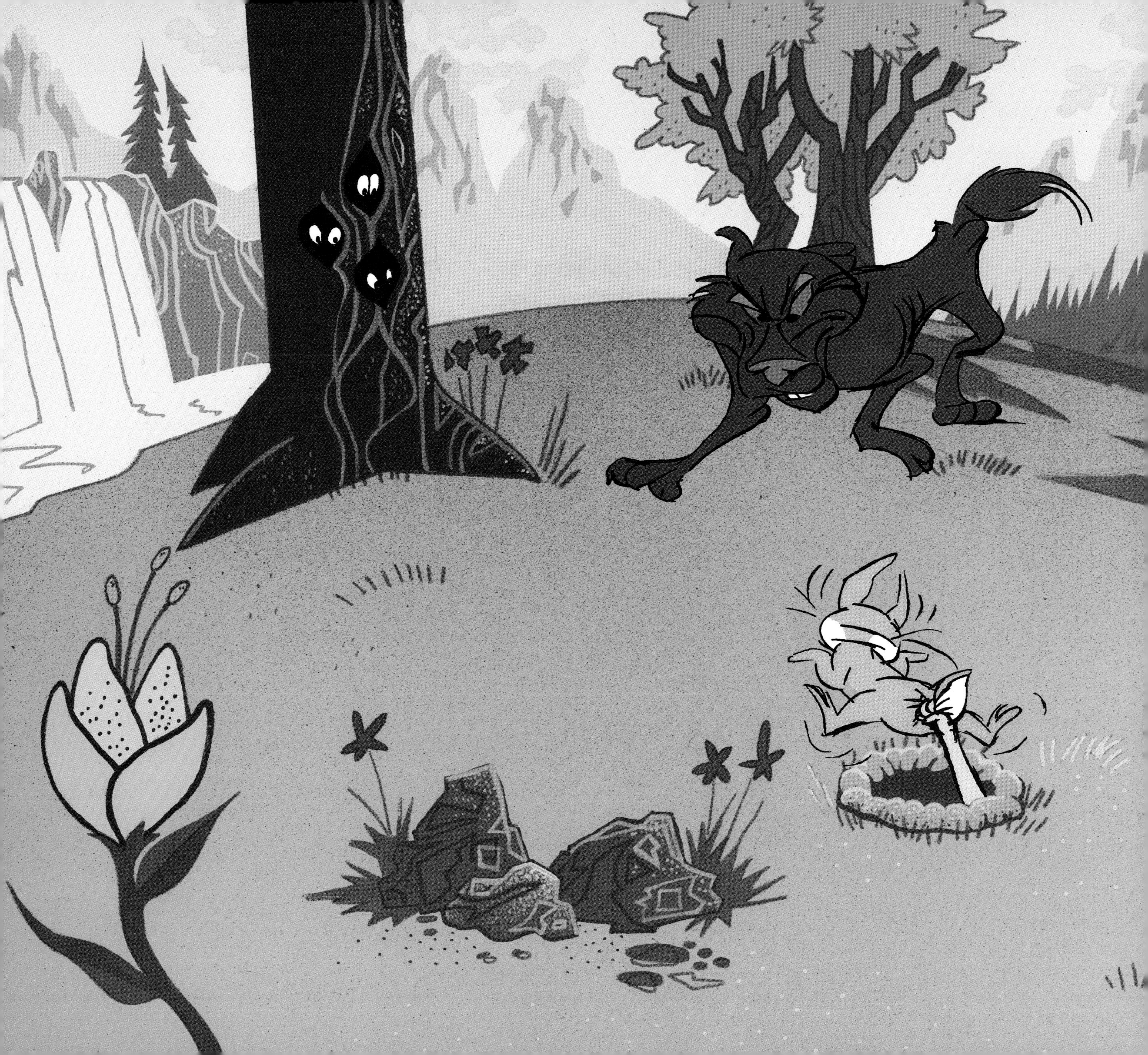

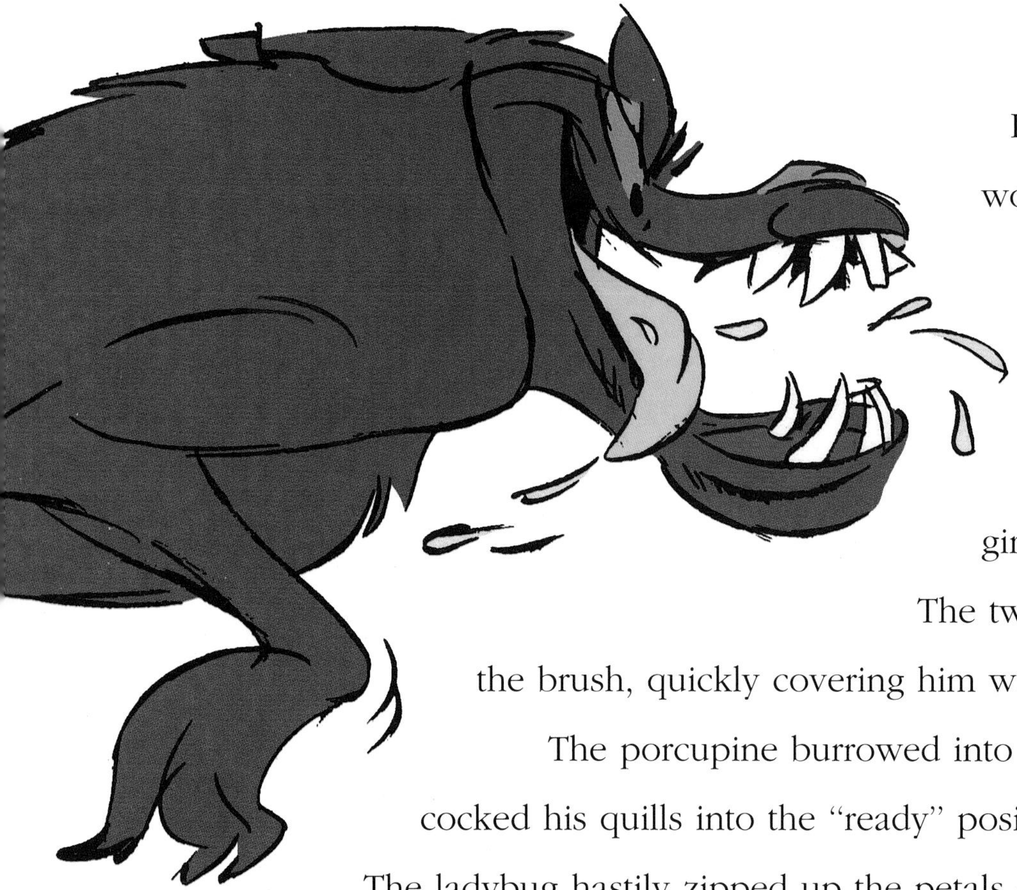

In a flash, all of the meadow reacted to the wolf's ominous presence.

The baby squirrels darted into the knothole at the base of the tree, followed by their mother.

The boy rabbit protectively pulled his girlfriend into a nearby rabbit hole.

The two deer nuzzled their fawn into the safety of the brush, quickly covering him with grass.

The porcupine burrowed into the tall reeds. (As an afterthought, he cocked his quills into the "ready" position.)

The ladybug hastily zipped up the petals of her morning glory.

Even the waterfall sensed danger and covered its eyes with its watery arms as the wolf passed.

Back at the base of the oak tree, the cat's tail stopped in midbeat. All the hair on its back rose up in fear at the sight of the wolf, who was wending his way past the oak tree at that very moment. In the blink of an eye, the cat scampered up the tree to safety.

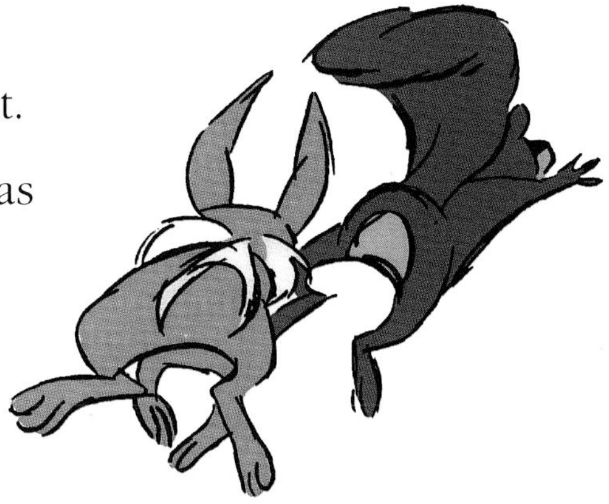

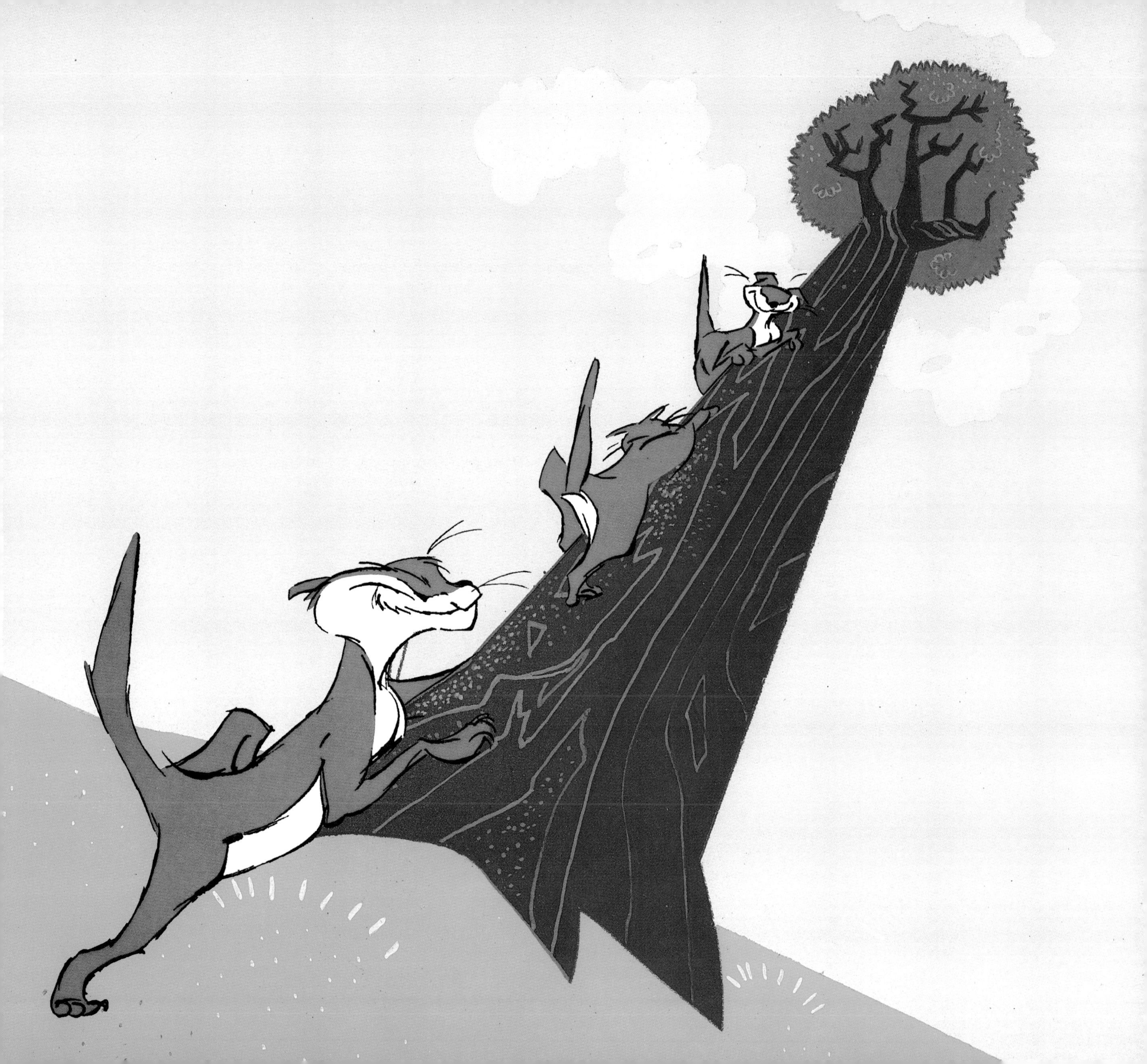

The wolf, however, did not even notice the cat. His appetite was whetted for duck, and he focused on his prey, still swimming in the middle of the pond.

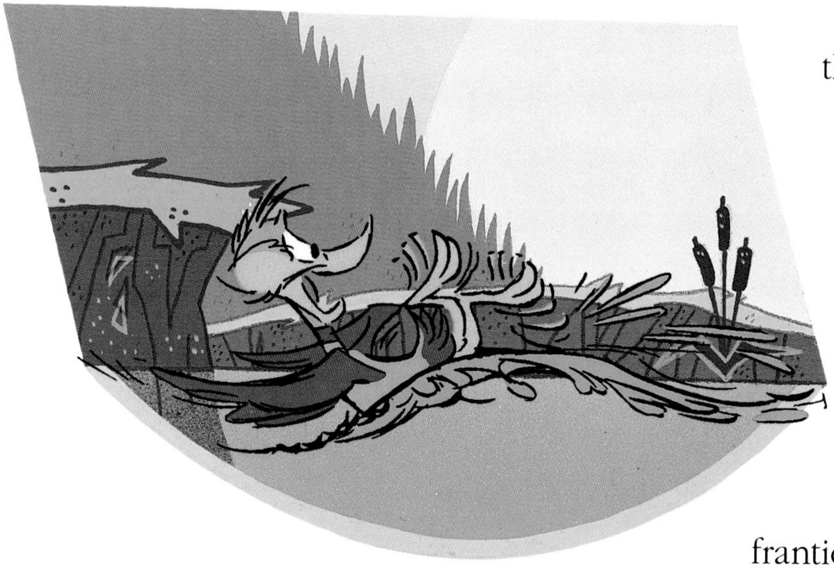

About this time, the duck awakened from the reverie of his leisurely swim and spotted the wolf stalking toward the water's edge. And, instead of staying right in the middle of the pond, where the wolf couldn't get him, the duck became so excited that he darted for the house, leaving the safety of the water. "Quack, quack, quack!" The duck made a frantic dash toward the cottage.

Meanwhile, the wolf, racing in dangerously large strides, got closer and closer and closer, moving in on the duck . . . who was still quacking for all he was worth, trying to get away.

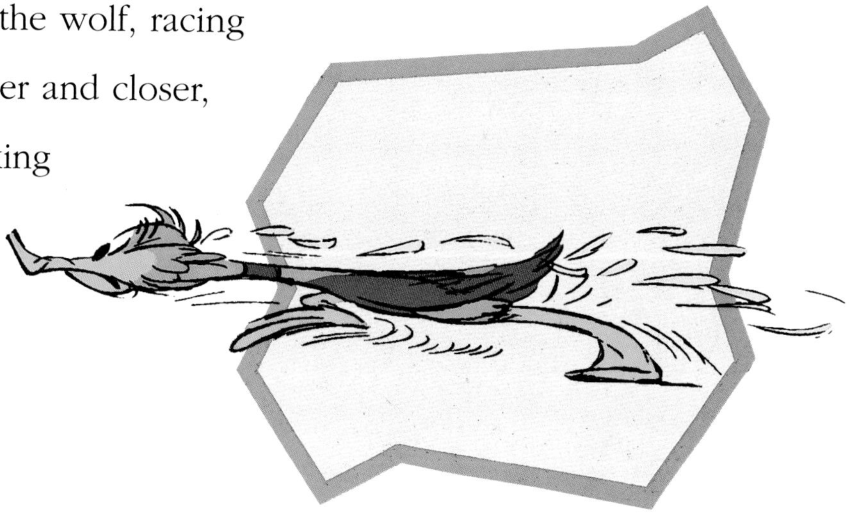

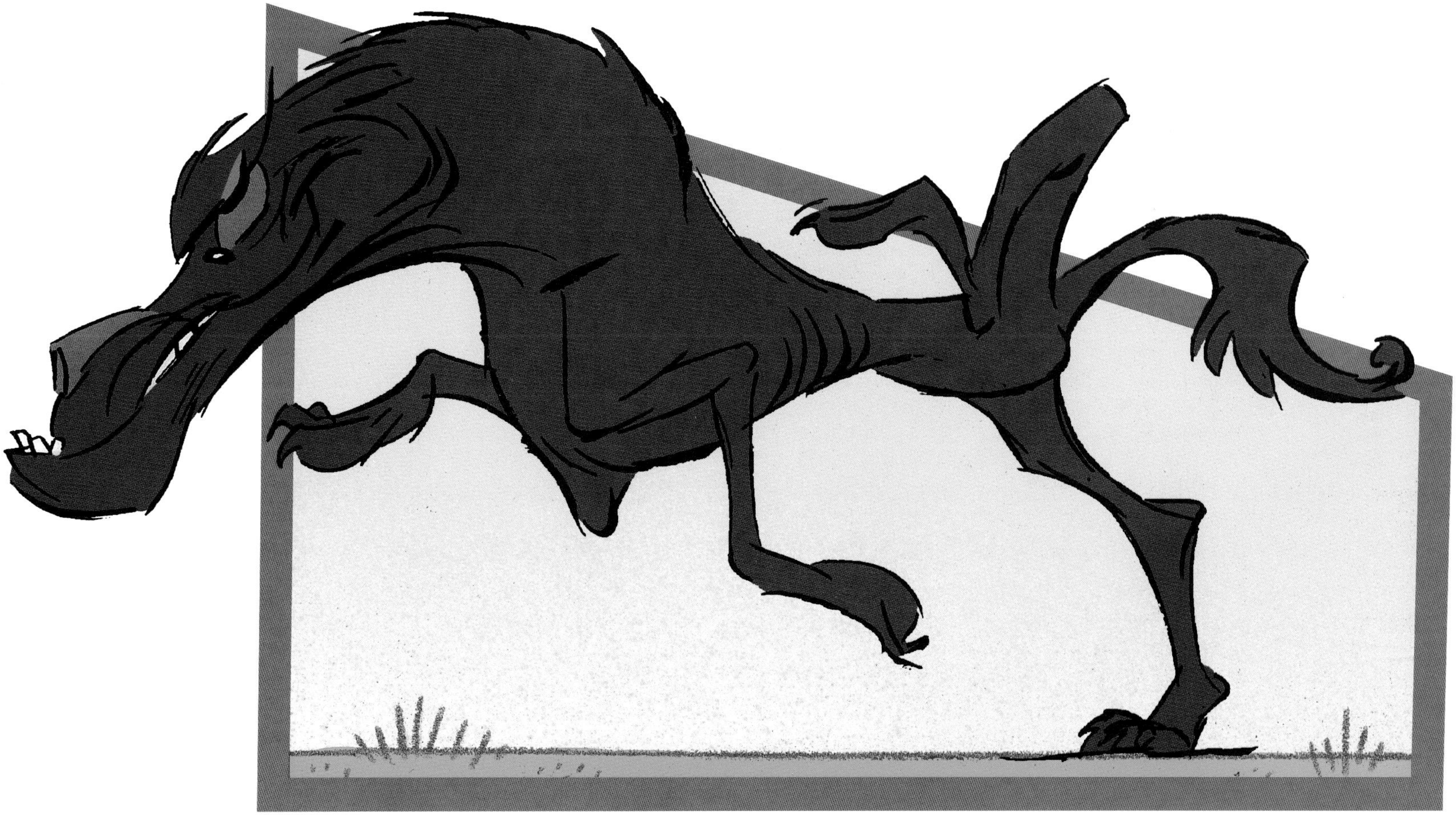

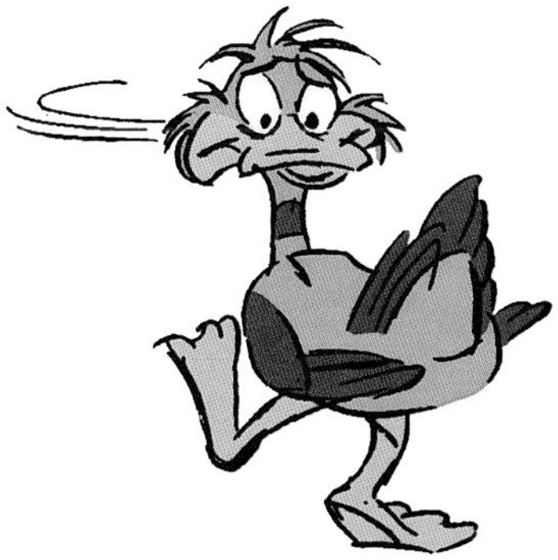

"Quack, quack, quack!" The duck cried even more frantically.

Closer and closer and closer the wolf came!

Then, all at once, he grabbed the duck.

And with one gulp, the wolf swallowed the duck whole.

In the quiet, still air, a lone duck feather fluttered to the earth on the whisper of a rippling breeze. The wolf licked his lips, smiled, and once again, his gold tooth glittered in the sunlight.

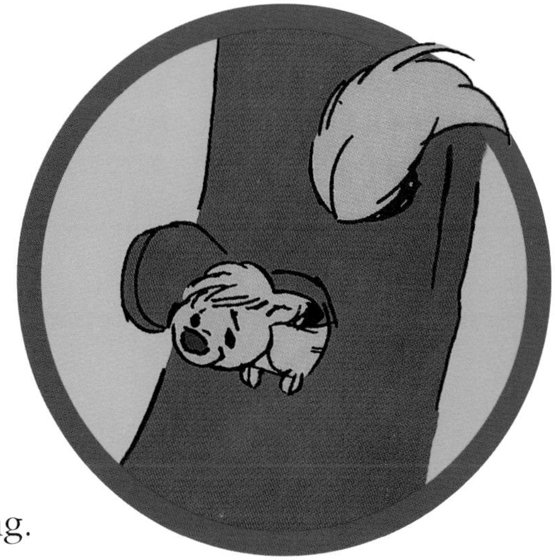

For a moment, the meadow was silent. Then, a cloud of sadness swept through the rolling hills, around the trees, and right over the flowers . . . just like a spring storm.

The little squirrels peeked out of their knothole, quivering.

The deer's eyes were moist with grief.

The rabbit hugged his mate protectively.

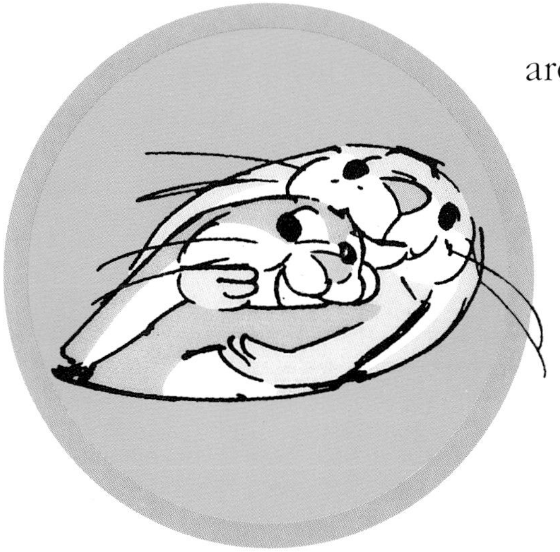

The ladybug tried to pull the morning glory tighter around her, but was shivering so much that the petals kept popping open.

The porcupine stared sadly at the wolf, his quills momentarily sagging.

Finally, the waterfall shed a tear.

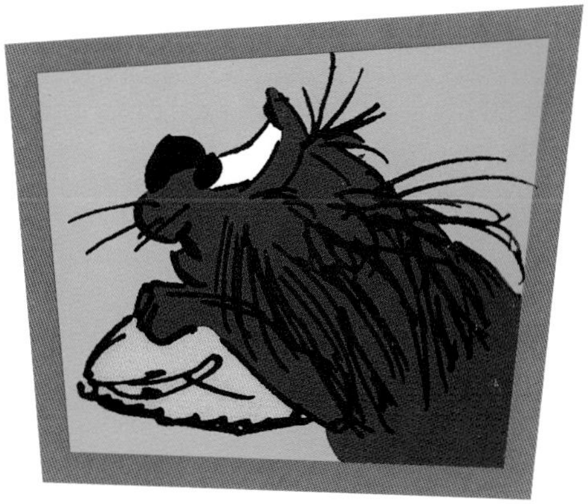

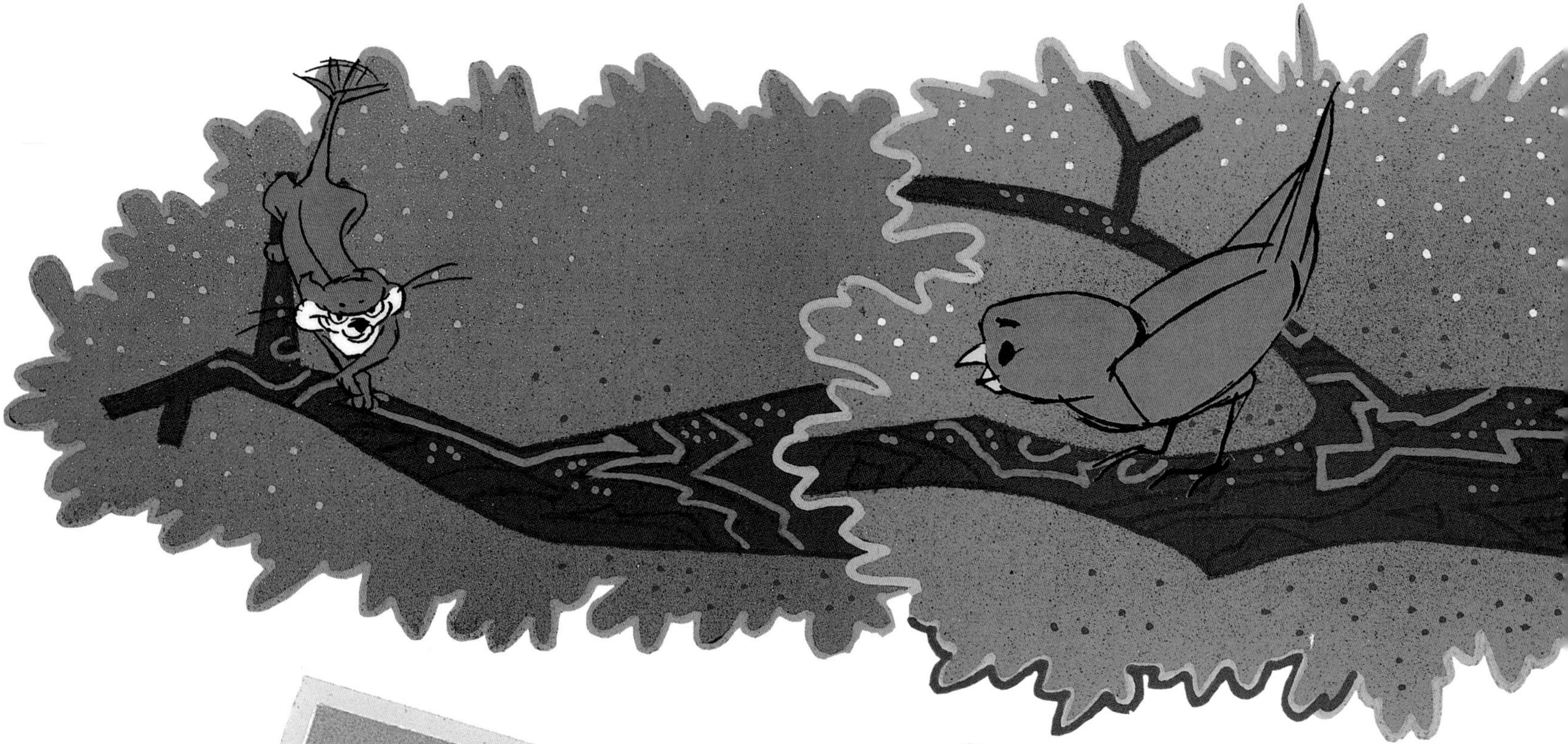

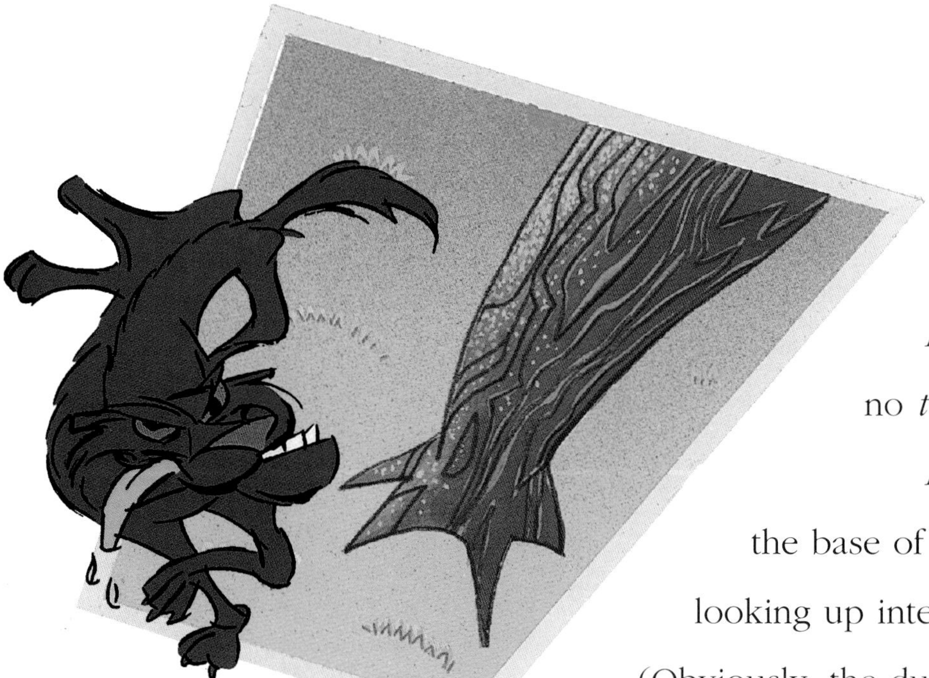

So, here's how things stood.

The cat was perched on one branch of the huge oak tree. And the bird was on another. (But no *too* close to the cat!)

And underneath, the wolf circled the base of the tree in a slow, deliberate arc, looking up intently at the cat and the bird. (Obviously, the duck had only been an appetizer!)

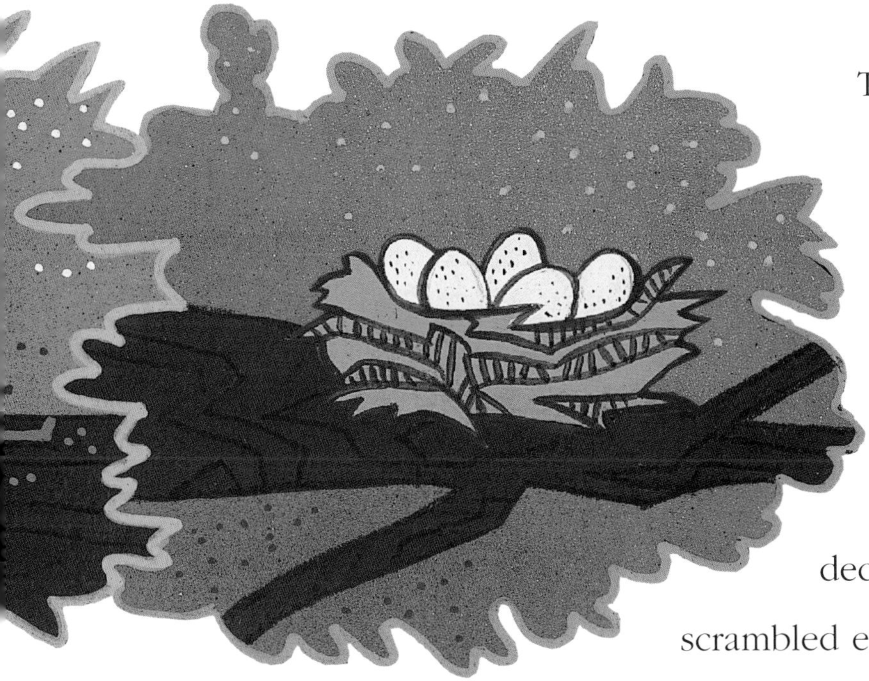

The bird guarded her nest protectively, keeping one eye on the wolf and one eye on the cat.

And although the cat's gaze seemed to be singularly transfixed on the wolf, the bird knew that a cat's attention span could be spontaneously fickle (in a distinctively feline way). Why, at any second, the cat could decide to calm his nerves with a quick meal of scrambled eggs.

So, the bird bore down on the cat with a stare so intent that he didn't even consider inching toward the nest.

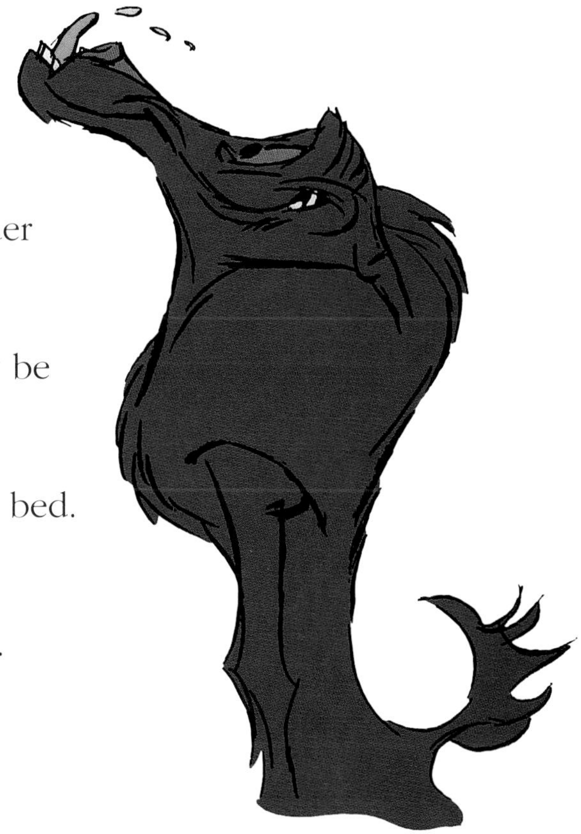

The cat, for his part, decided that he had experienced just about enough of this first day of spring. After all, just under him paced a voraciously hungry wolf. And to his left was an overwrought, hysterical bird who, he thought, could probably be just as troublesome as the wolf.

"Tomorrow," thought the cat, "I'm staying under Peter's bed. From now on, I'm a house cat."

Meanwhile, the wolf observed the goings-on in the tree.

So did Peter.

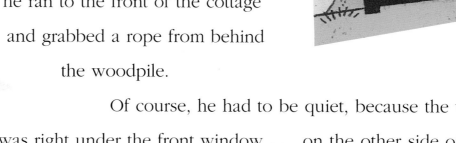

Without showing the slightest bit of fear, Peter had watched the entire scene unfold from behind the closed gate. For a moment, he analyzed the situation. Then, he ran to the front of the cottage and grabbed a rope from behind the woodpile.

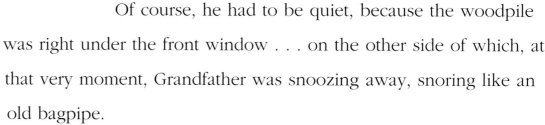

Of course, he had to be quiet, because the woodpile was right under the front window . . . on the other side of which, at that very moment, Grandfather was snoozing away, snoring like an old bagpipe.

Peter did not want to wake Grandfather. Another lecture was the *last* thing he needed at this critical moment.

So, Peter silently crept away from the window. He held the rope tightly by his side and expertly climbed up on top of the high stone wall that separated the cottage from the meadow.

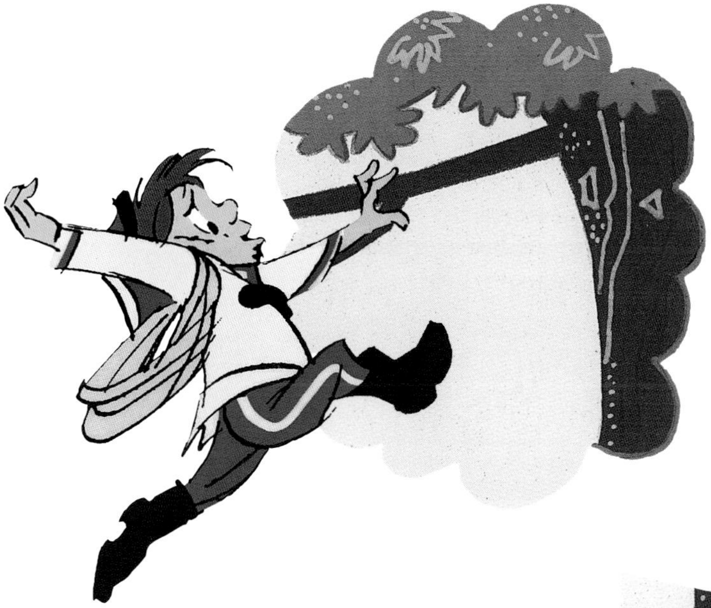

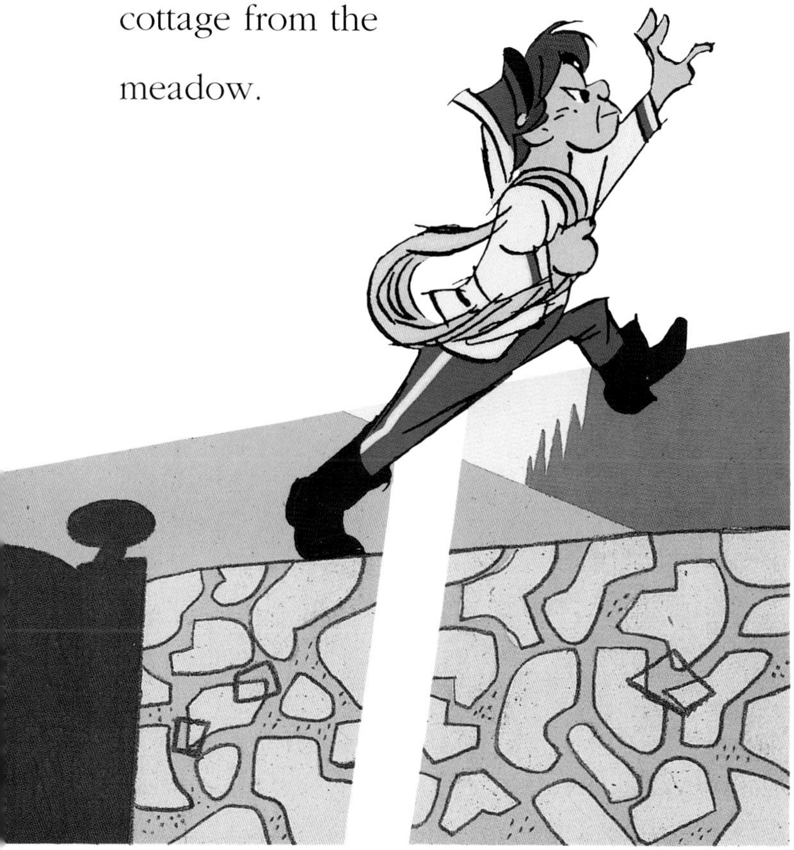

He swung onto the giant overhanging branch, and moved silently through the leaves, quietly shimmying down the tree into the meadow.

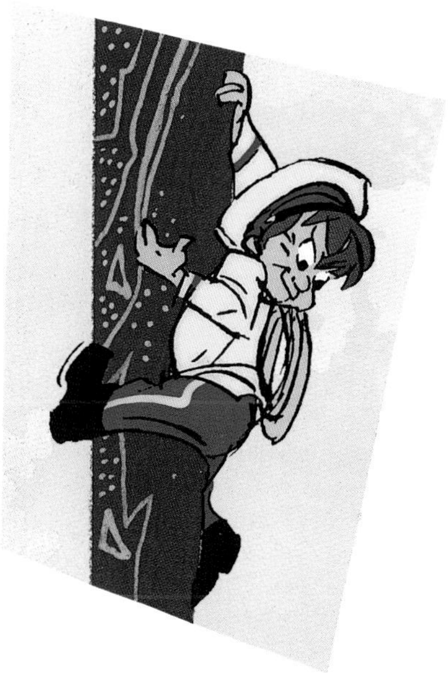

Then, with a deep breath and a determined shake of his head, he bravely began to sneak through the meadow. Through the tall grass and willows, Peter silently crept, making quite sure he wasn't seen by anyone.

Not by Grandfather.

And especially, not by the wolf.

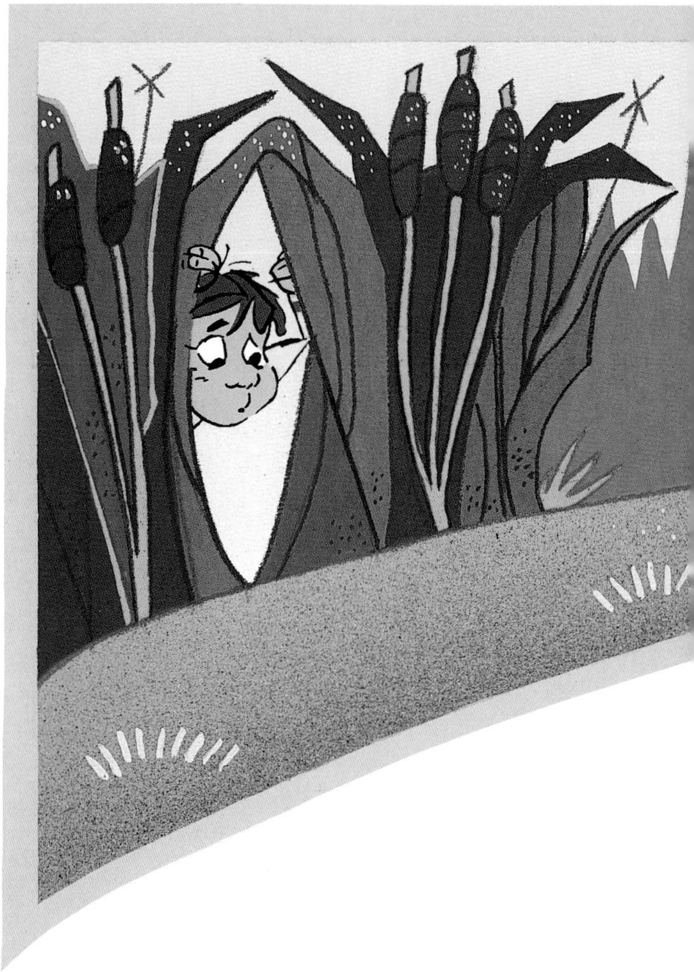

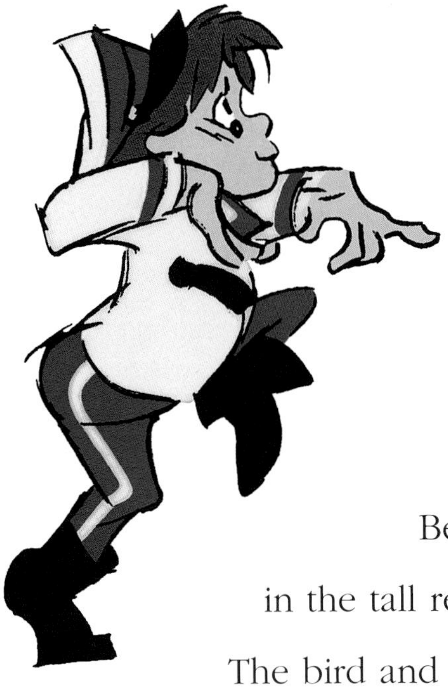

Before long, Peter arrived at the pond's bank. From his hiding place in the tall reeds, he could see everything.

The bird and the cat were still in the tree, and the wolf was still circling at the bottom, planning the next two courses of his midday menu.

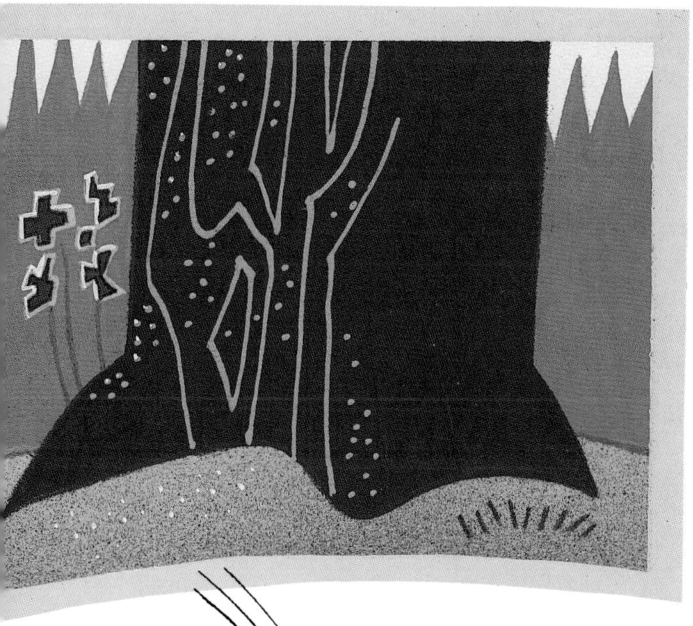

Peter decided that a little diversion might be just what his battle plan needed.

He spotted a rock on the ground and quickly threw it into the pond.

Splash.

The wolf rushed over to the water to see what new gastronomic delight might be paddling around in the water.

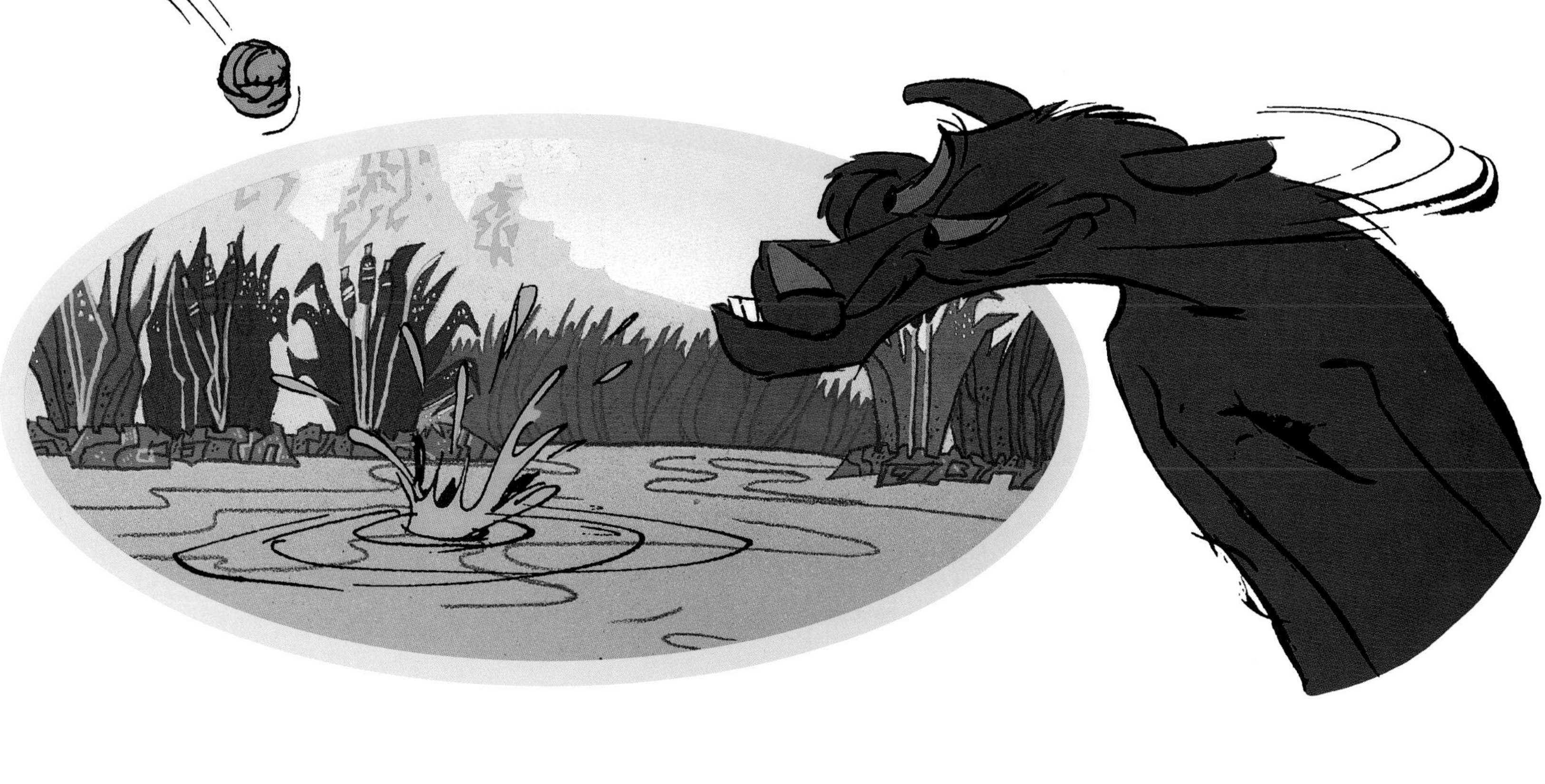

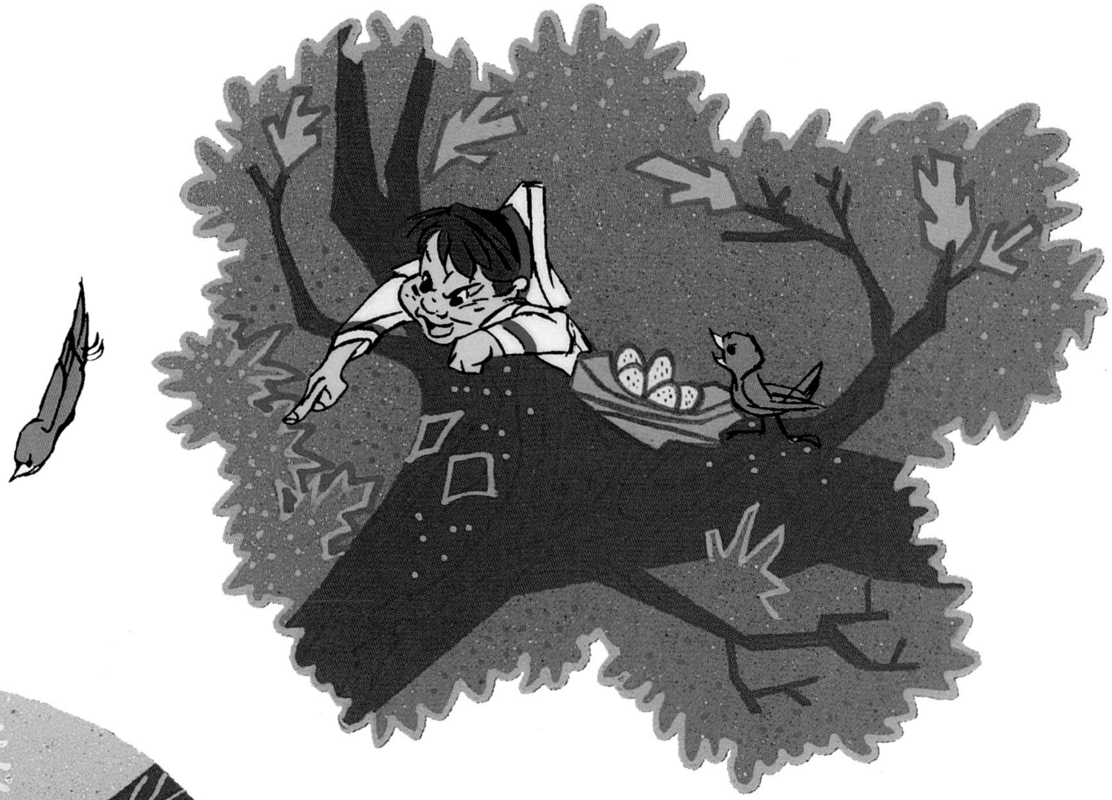

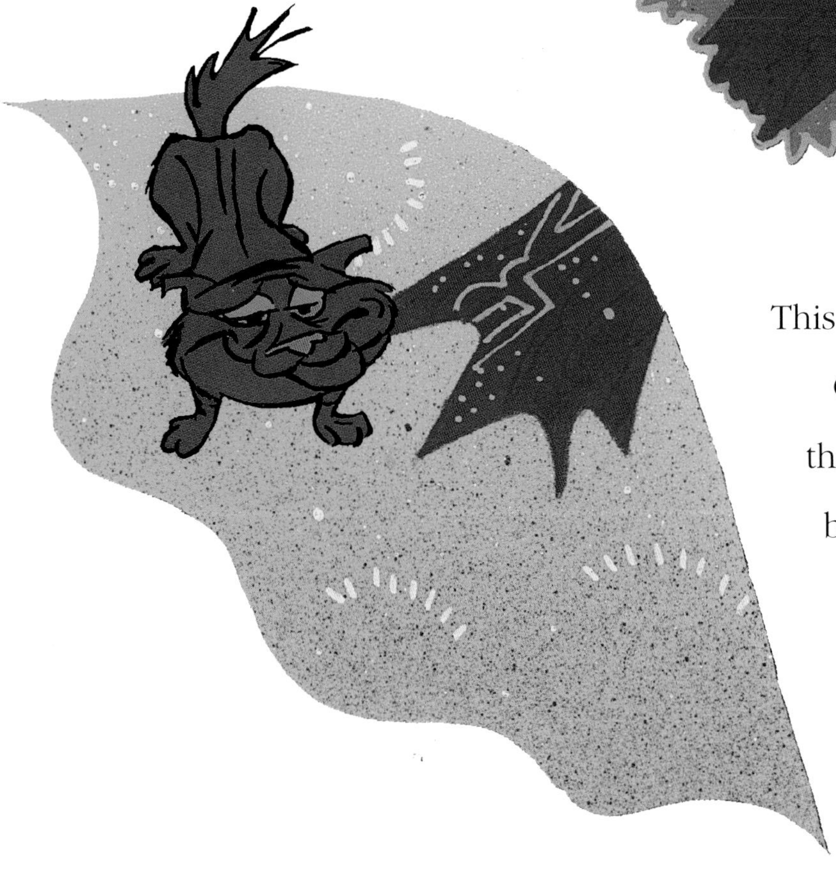

This gave Peter the chance to climb the tree.

Quickly and quietly, he climbed to the top of the leafy branches and edged over next to the bird.

"Fly down and circle the wolf's head. I've got a plan," he told the bird. "Don't blow it. That wolf has it *bad* for birds!"

Without the slightest hesitation, the bird did exactly what Peter asked. In a dazzling display of avian choreography, she soared and darted and dove around the wolf's head.

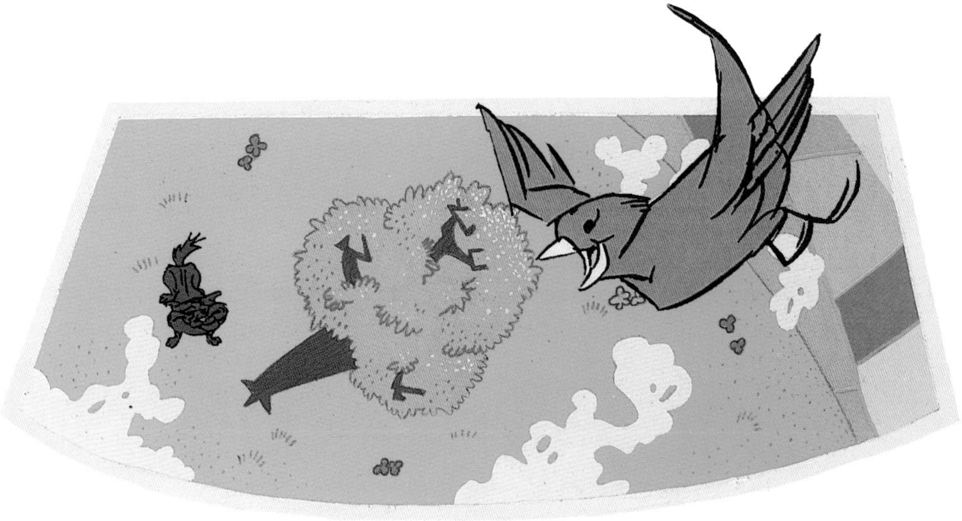

Peter was impressed. Even the cat was impressed, for the bird's flying skills were unbelievable. She zoomed and banked and executed dizzying spins and triple rollovers around the shell-shocked wolf's ears.

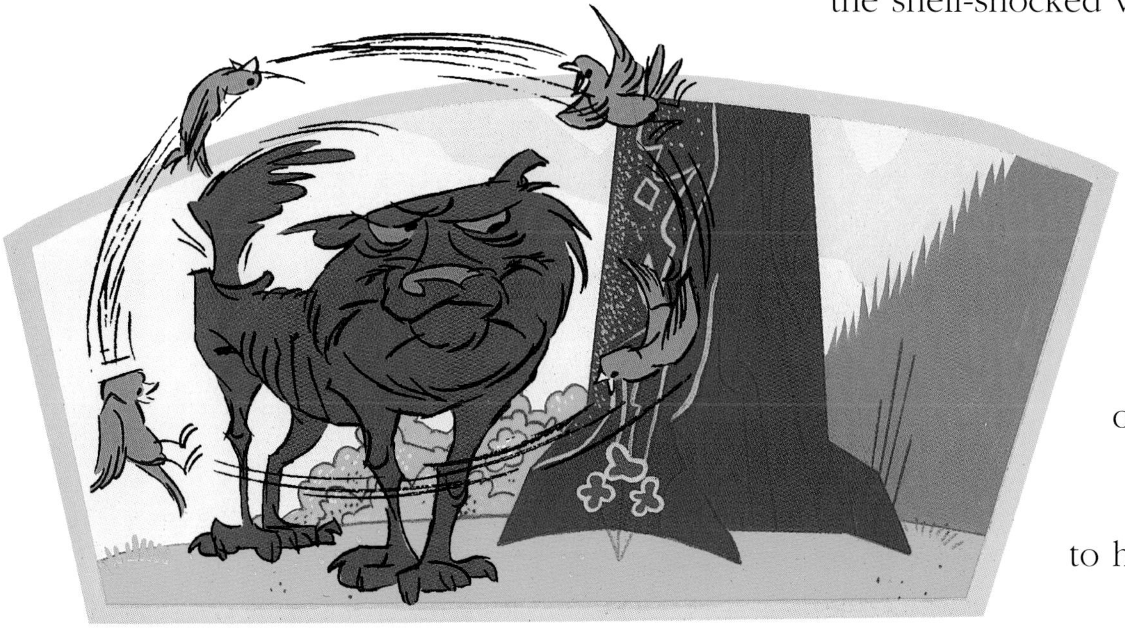

At first, the wolf was so stunned by this feathery bombardment that he didn't even attempt to catch her. He just tried to stay out of the way.

But the wolf quickly came to his senses.

His eyes glowed red, and he prepared to go in for the kill.

Snap! Snap! The wolf lunged at the bird.

But he missed. For the bird was way too quick and agile.

Snap! Snap! The wolf tried again.

And again he missed.

Undaunted, the bird continued her aerial assault on the wolf. This time, she led him in a circle . . . around and around and around. And the wolf followed her, ending up chasing his tail like a dizzy little puppy. Suddenly, the wolf realized what he was doing, and caught himself with a sheepish gasp.

Now, he was furious. No bird was going to make a fool out of the king of the forest. He resumed his attack.

Snap! Snap! Once again, another miss.

Snap! Snap!

Snap! Snap!

Snap! Snap!

The wolf continually missed. He just could not get the bird. In truth, he never did stand a chance, for the bird was way too clever and way too fast.

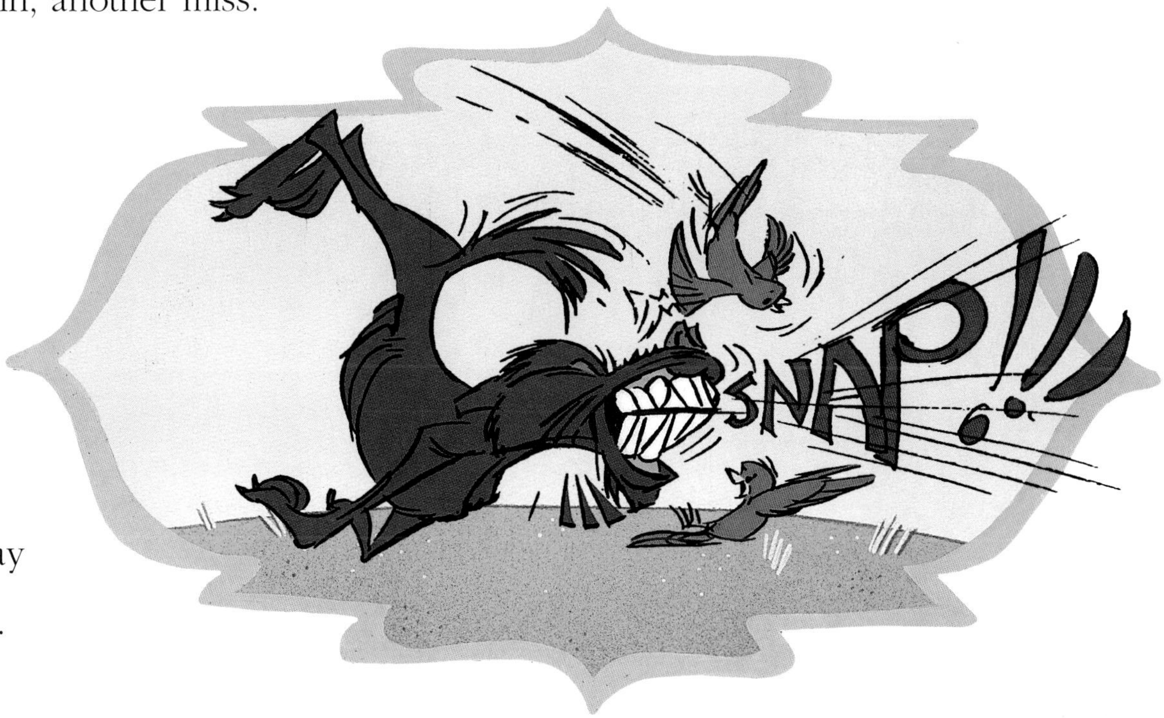
SNAP!!!

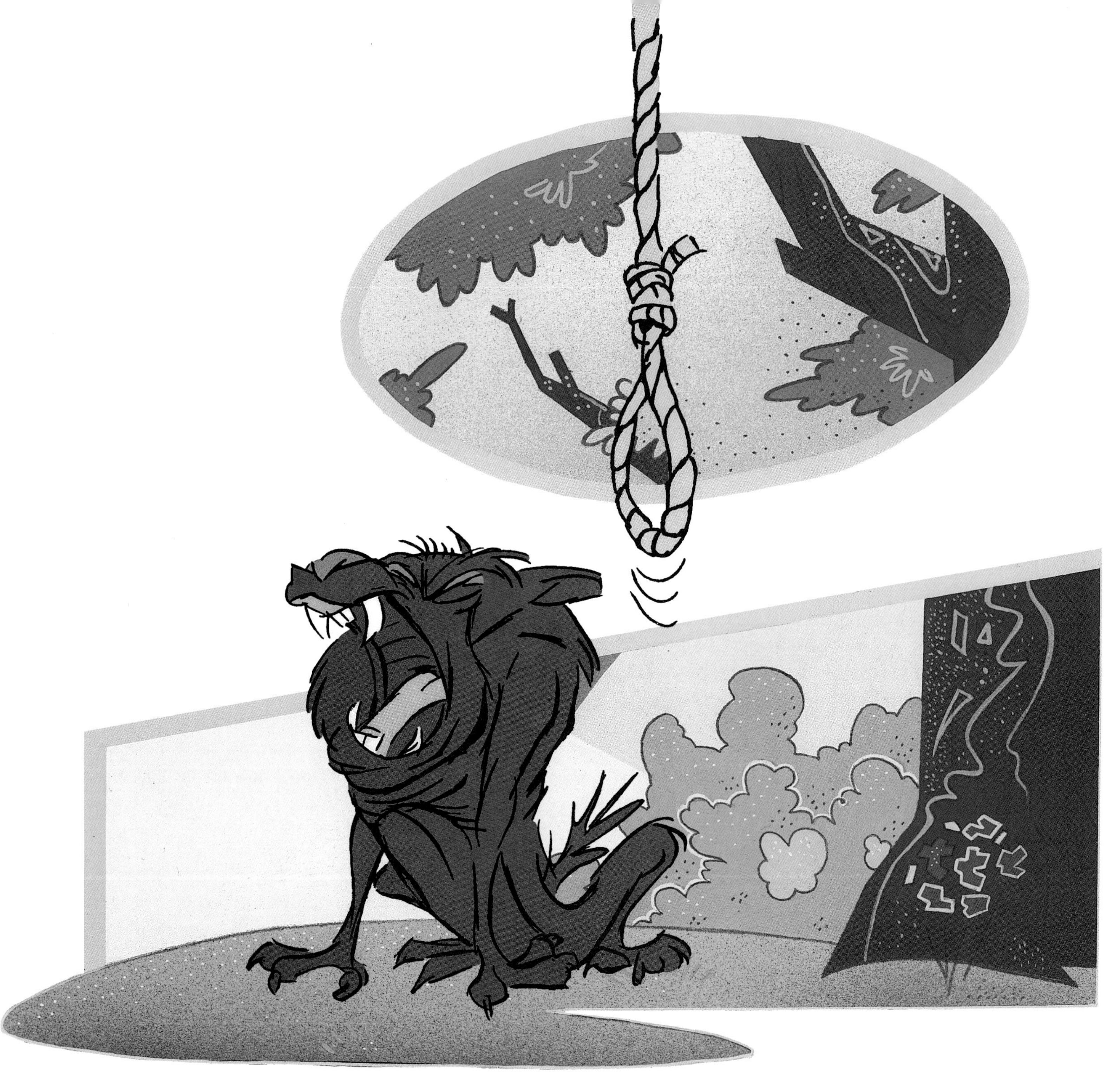

Finally, in momentary defeat, and no doubt exhaustion, the wolf gave up.

"Yawn!" he sighed.

He slumped onto the ground at the base of the tree and decided to take a quick nap before continuing on to the next course of his lunch. While dreaming visions of sugarplummed cat and fricasseed bird, the wolf drifted off into a delicious sleep.

Little did the wolf realize that a rope was slowly navigating its way down through the very tree he was snoozing under.

Silently and steadily, guided by Peter's
confident head, the twine slithered to the
ground like a snake, gently wrapping
itself around the wolf's tail.

Then, fast as lightning,

Peter tugged on the rope.

Which, of course, awakened the wolf.

The wolf jumped violently, trying to free his tail from the rope's noose.
But the more he jumped and tugged, the tighter the rope became. He jumped so wildly, and was
so strong, that he shook the entire tree.

The tree swayed dramatically from left to right and back again, and the cat had to hold
tight and dig his claws into his branch in order to stay on his perch. The bird covered her eggs
with her wings to keep them from toppling out of the nest.

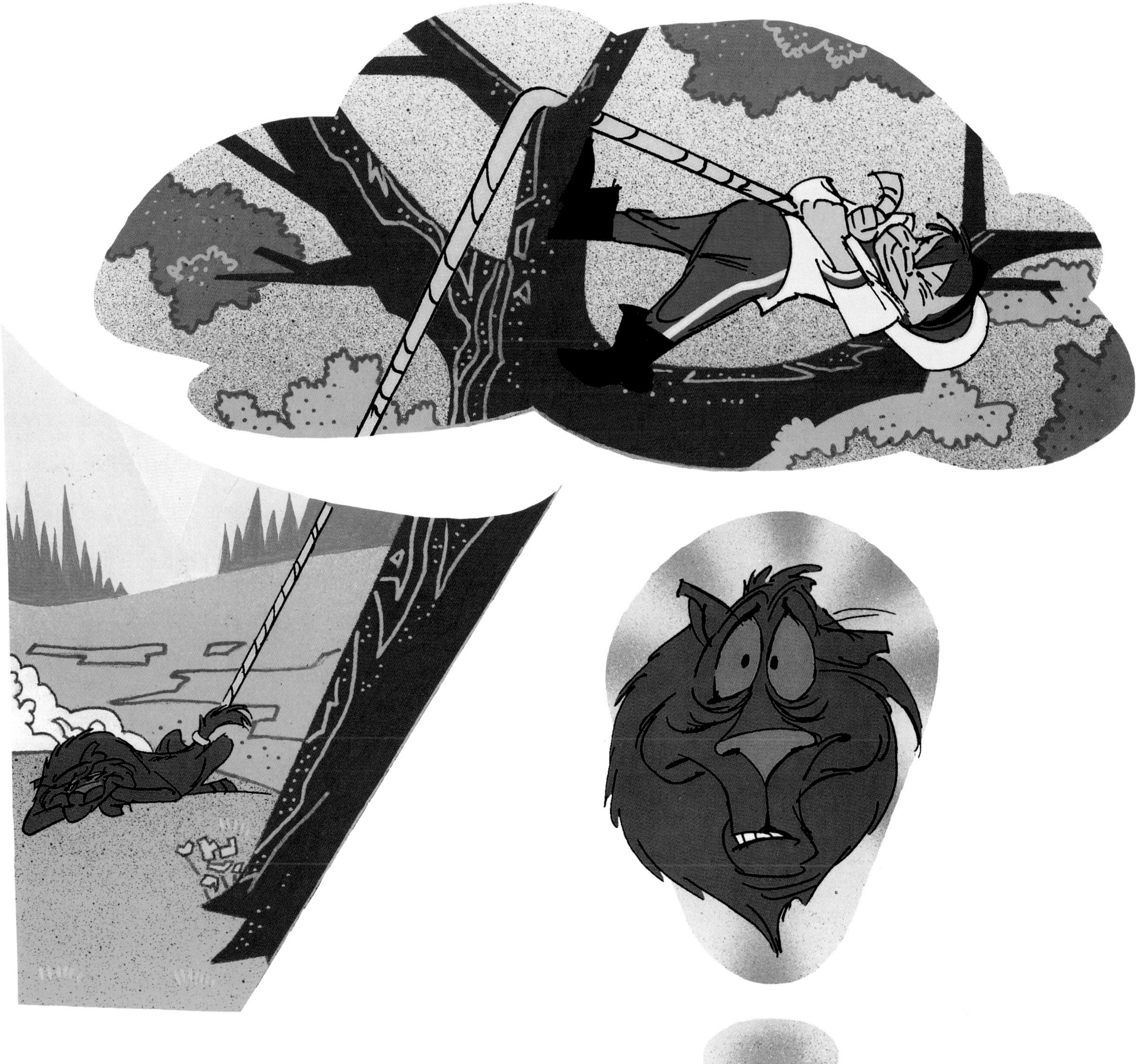

Meanwhile, the coolheaded Peter continued to tug on the rope with all of his might. He was determined to catch the wolf by pulling him up into the tree.

But the wolf was very strong and very, very heavy. And Peter was having trouble making any progress at all.

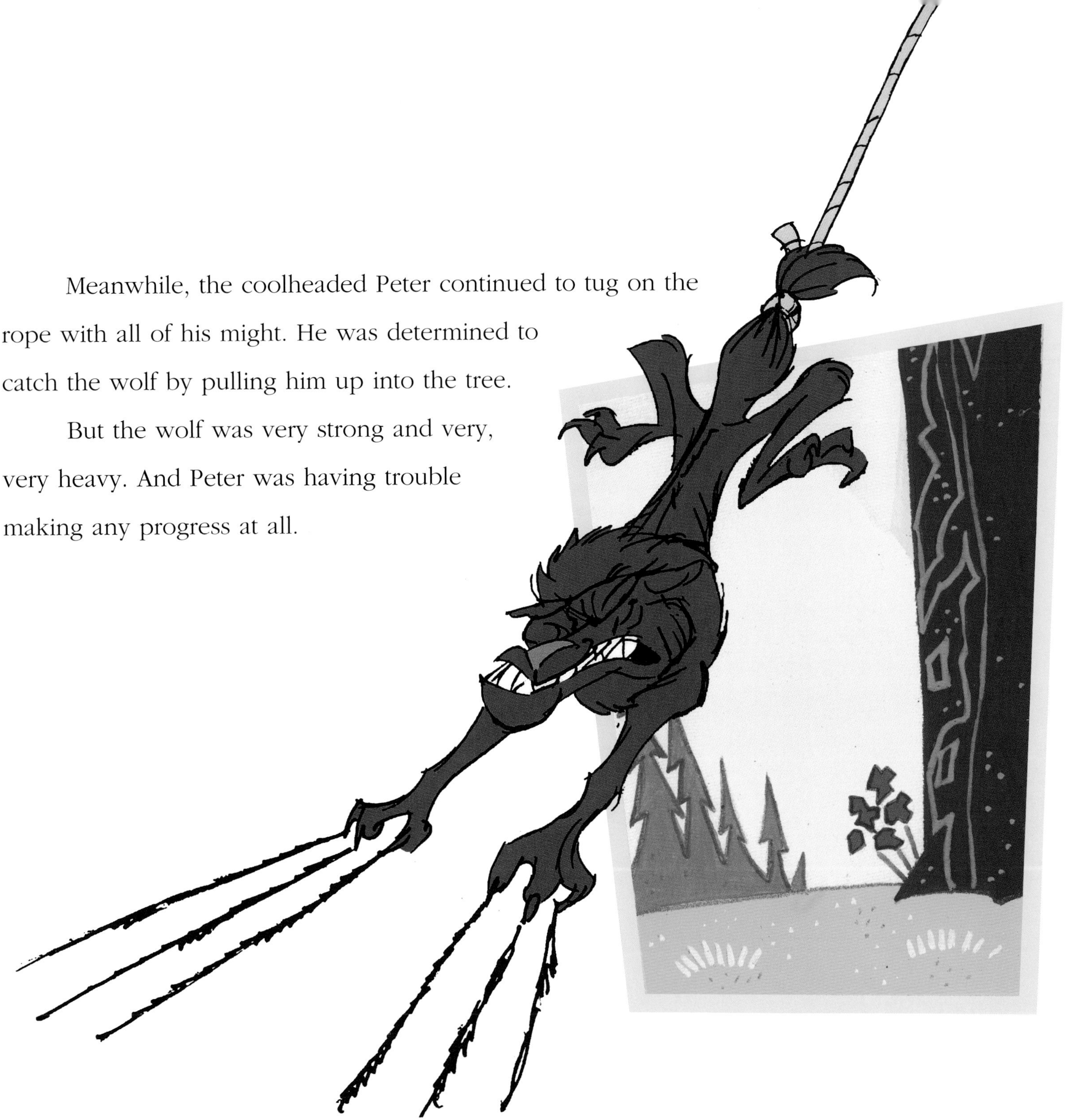

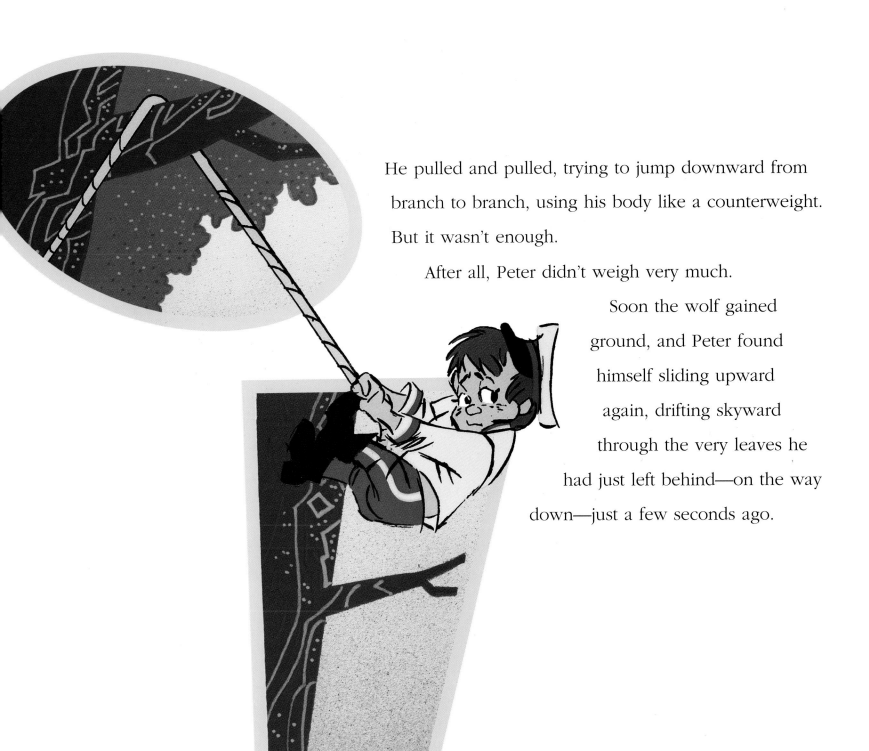

He pulled and pulled, trying to jump downward from branch to branch, using his body like a counterweight. But it wasn't enough.

After all, Peter didn't weigh very much.

Soon the wolf gained ground, and Peter found himself sliding upward again, drifting skyward through the very leaves he had just left behind—on the way down—just a few seconds ago.

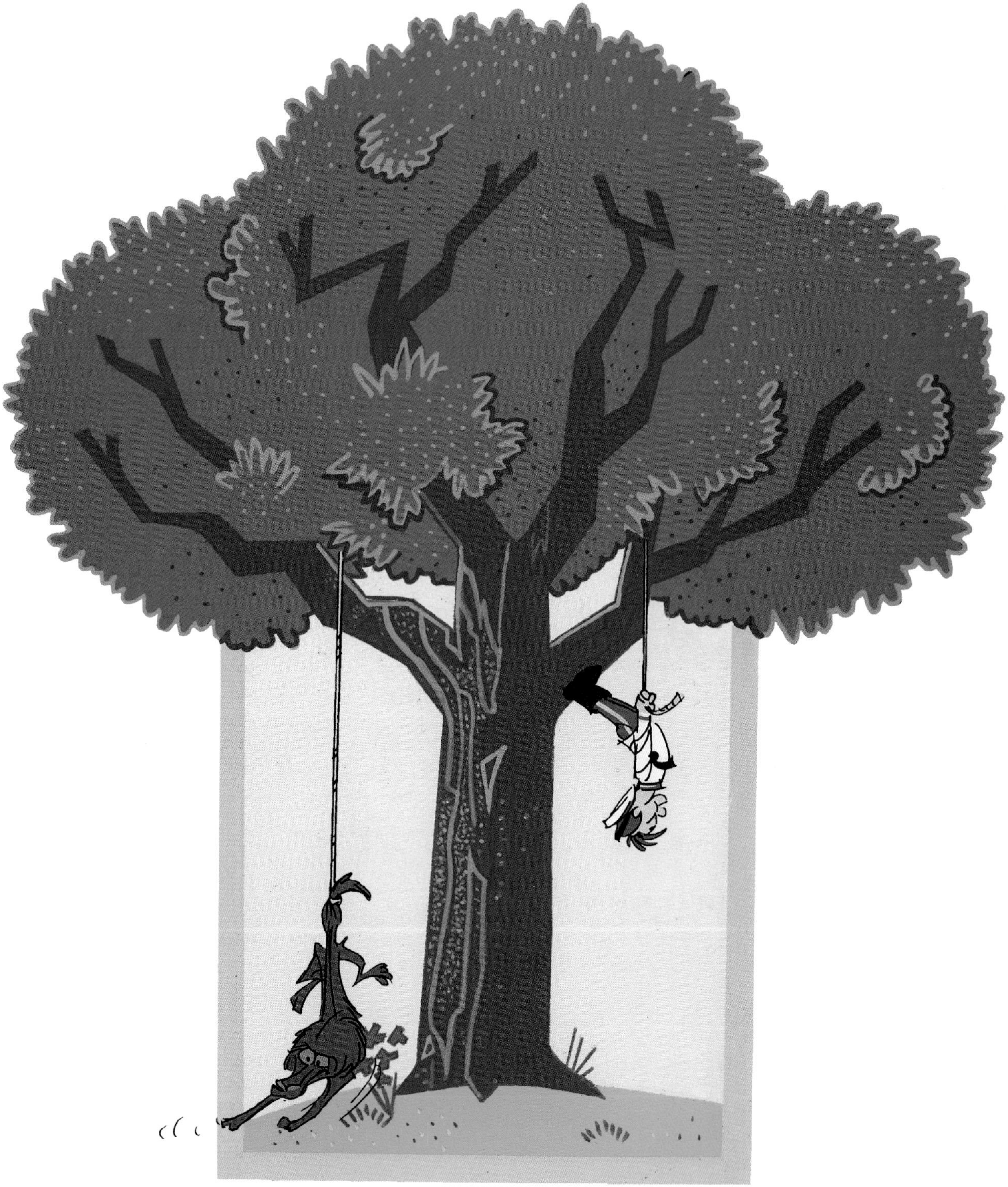

Back and forth it went, this battle between Peter and the wolf.

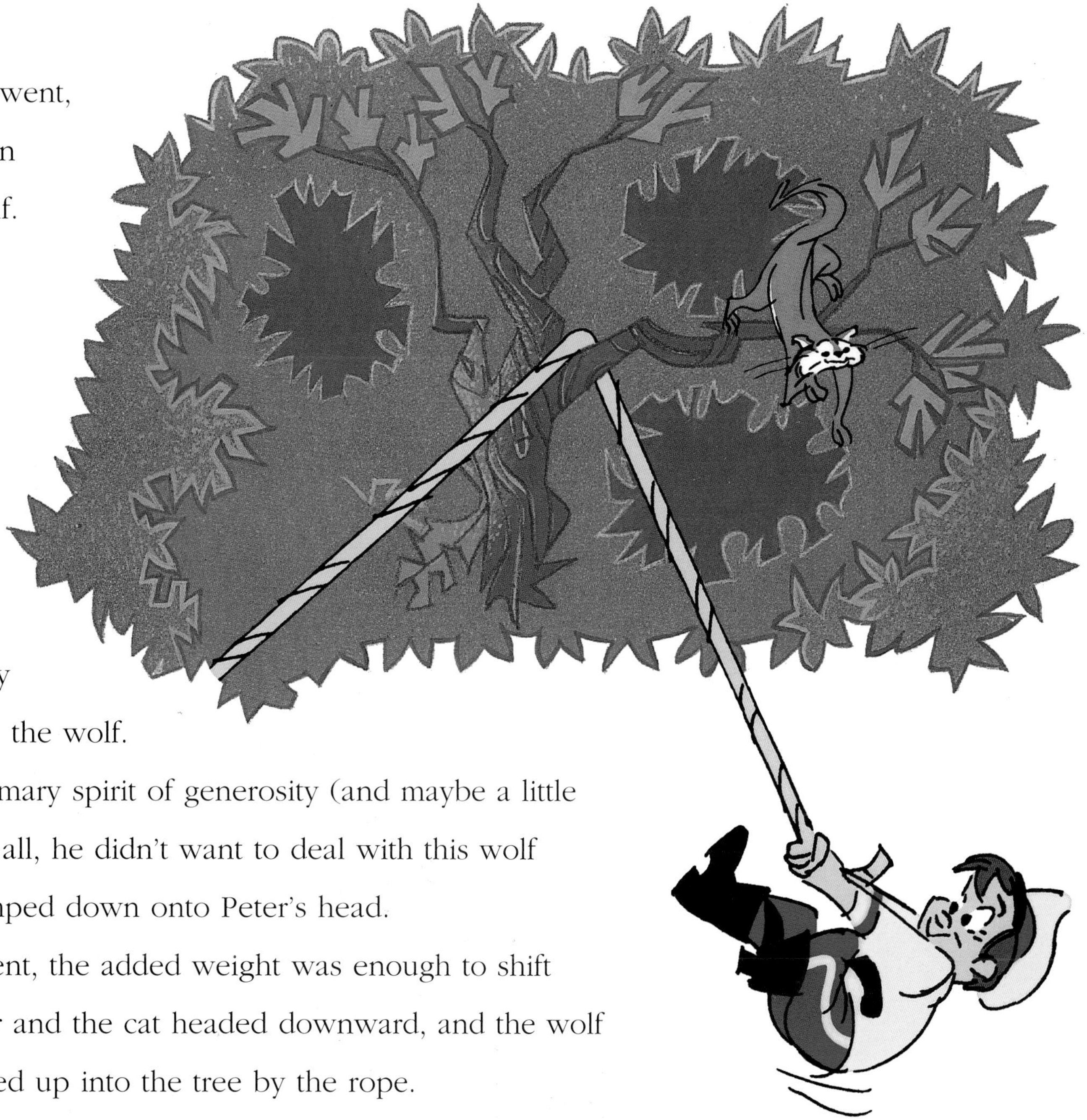

The cat watched from his vantage point in the tree and quickly realized that Peter wasn't big enough—or heavy enough—to snare the wolf. So, in an uncustomary spirit of generosity (and maybe a little selfishness—after all, he didn't want to deal with this wolf again) the cat jumped down onto Peter's head.

For a moment, the added weight was enough to shift the balance. Peter and the cat headed downward, and the wolf started to be pulled up into the tree by the rope.

But the wolf dug in his heels—
or was it his paws?—
and fought back.

Back up they went, Peter and the cat.

"Well," decided the bird, "they're never going to get this over with without me."

And with another flutter of her wings, the bird soared down and lit on top of the cat, who was

already perched on top of Peter. It was just enough to tip the scales, and downward they sailed,

this brave trio of Peter, the cat, and the bird.

bird

+

cat

+

Peter

Finally, Peter, with the help of his two friends, mustered all of his strength and gave one last gigantic pull. The wolf was pulled up into the tree, and in total and utter disbelief, the former bully found himself dangling from a branch by his tail—caught!

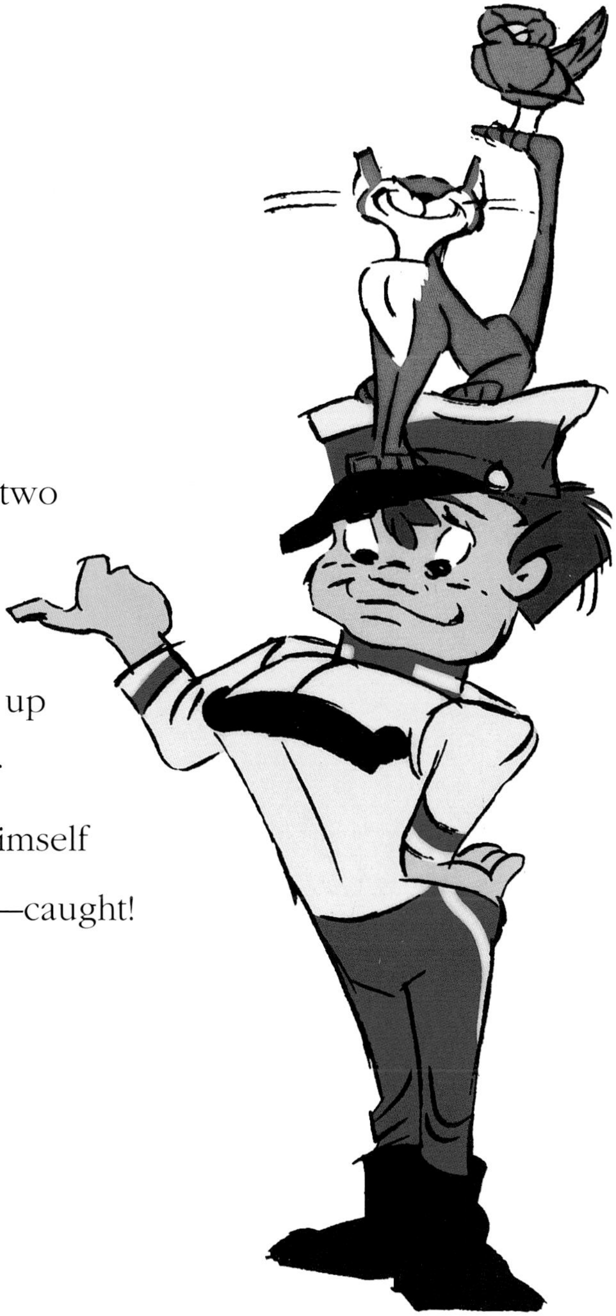

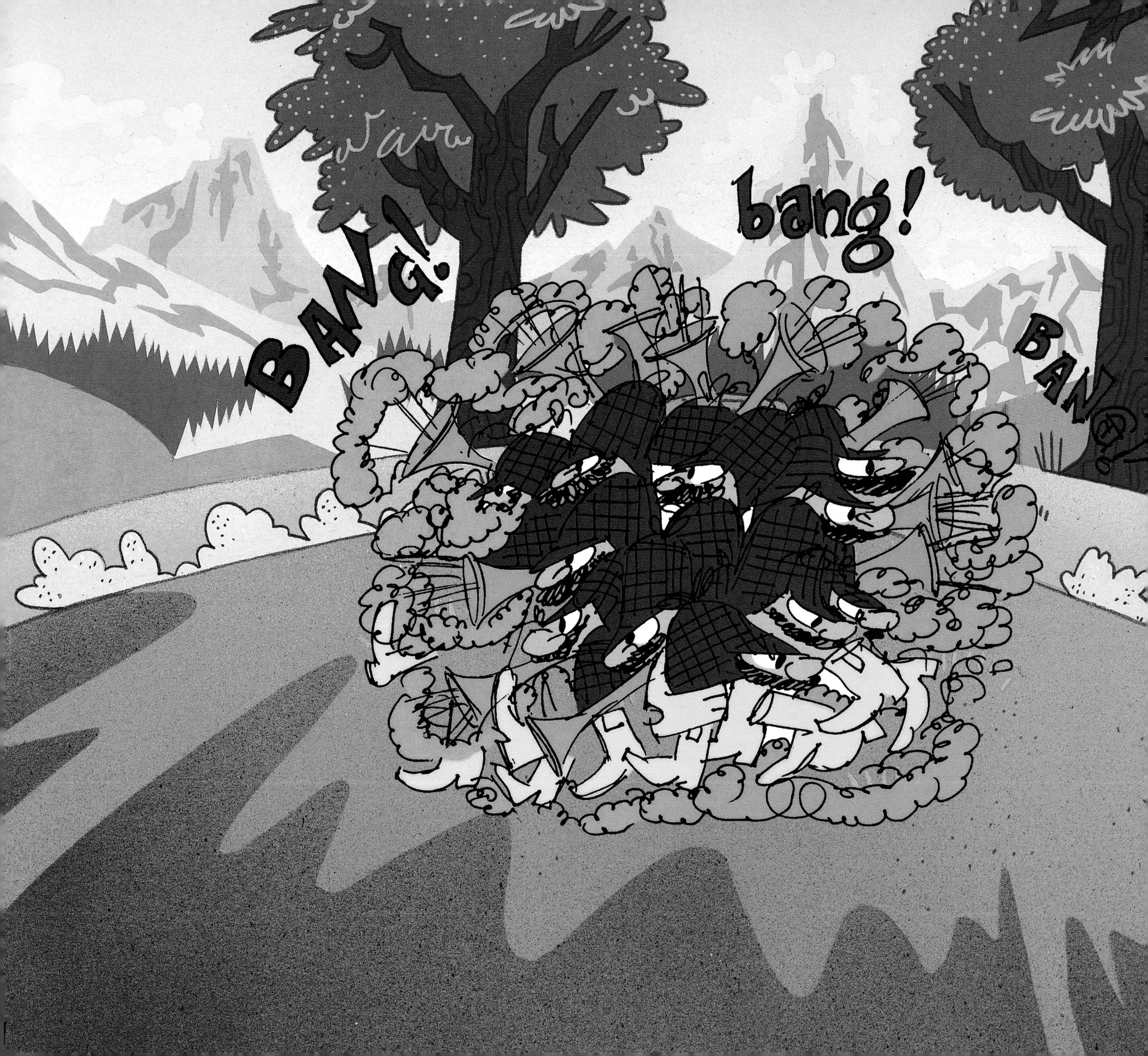
BANG!
bang!
BANG!

Just then, a flash of red and a puff of smoke appeared way off in the distance. A band of hunters rolled out of the woods and into the meadow. You see, the hunters had been following the wolf's trail.

Now, the hunters were a bumbling bunch, moving in march step amid a blur of red hats, white eyes, and yellow boots, all melding into one gigantically confused concoction of singular locomotion.

When they caught sight of the wolf's tracks, they became so excited that their guns accidentally went off in an impromptu twenty-one-gun salute.

They came closer, and actually spotted the wolf dangling from the tree.

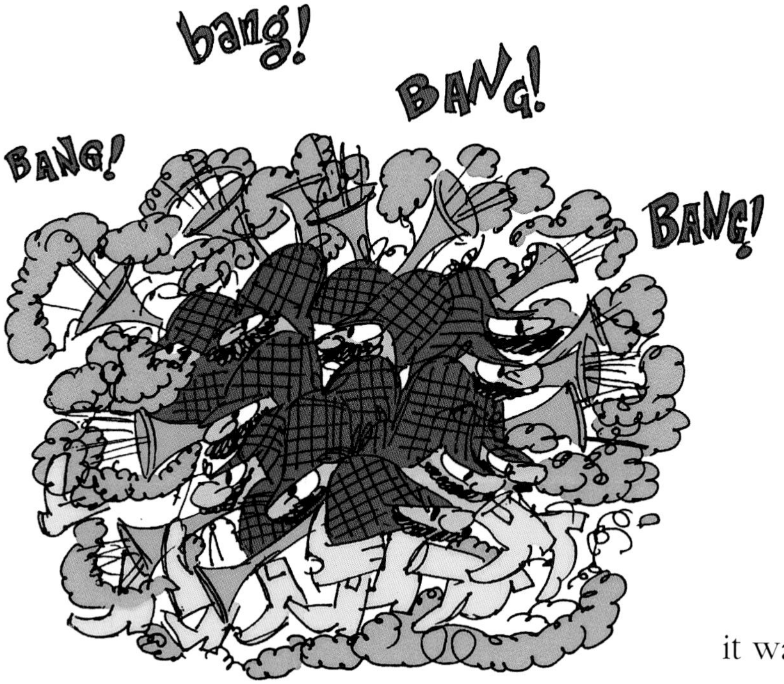
bang!
BANG!
BANG!
BANG!

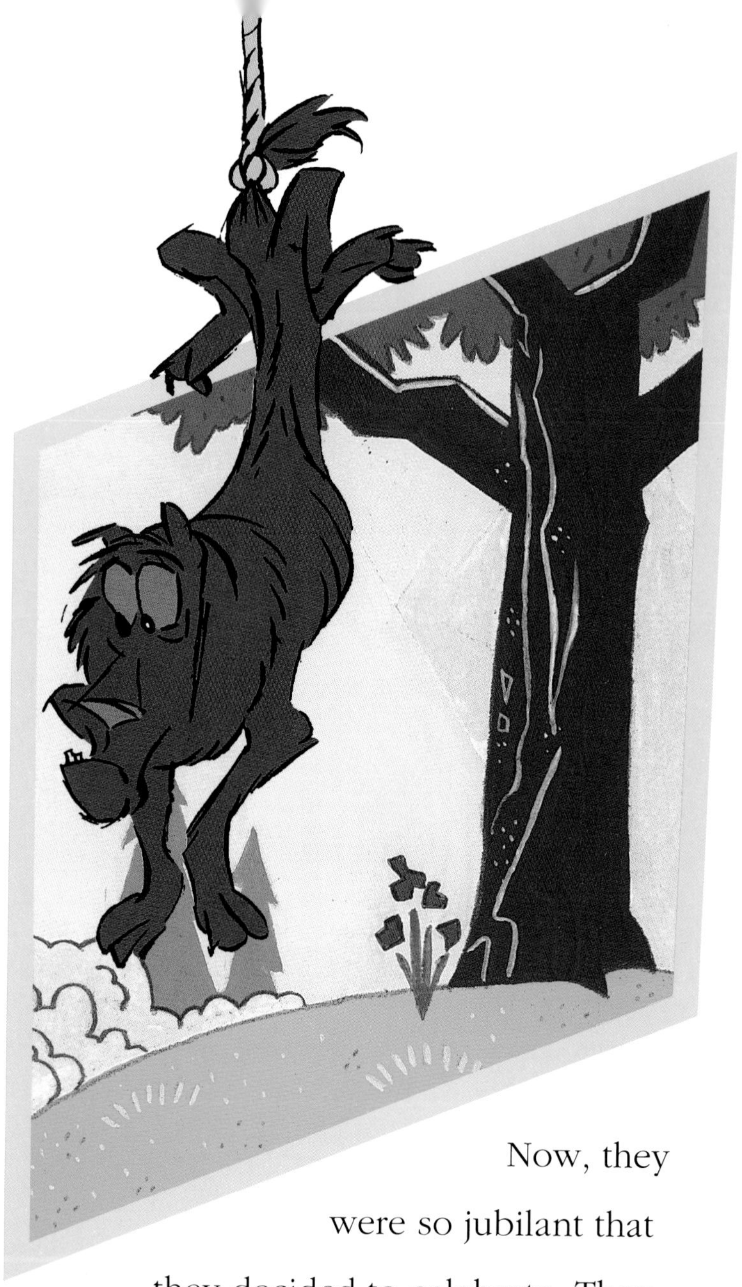

Now, they were so jubilant that they decided to celebrate. They fired a volley of shots into the air. This time it was on purpose.

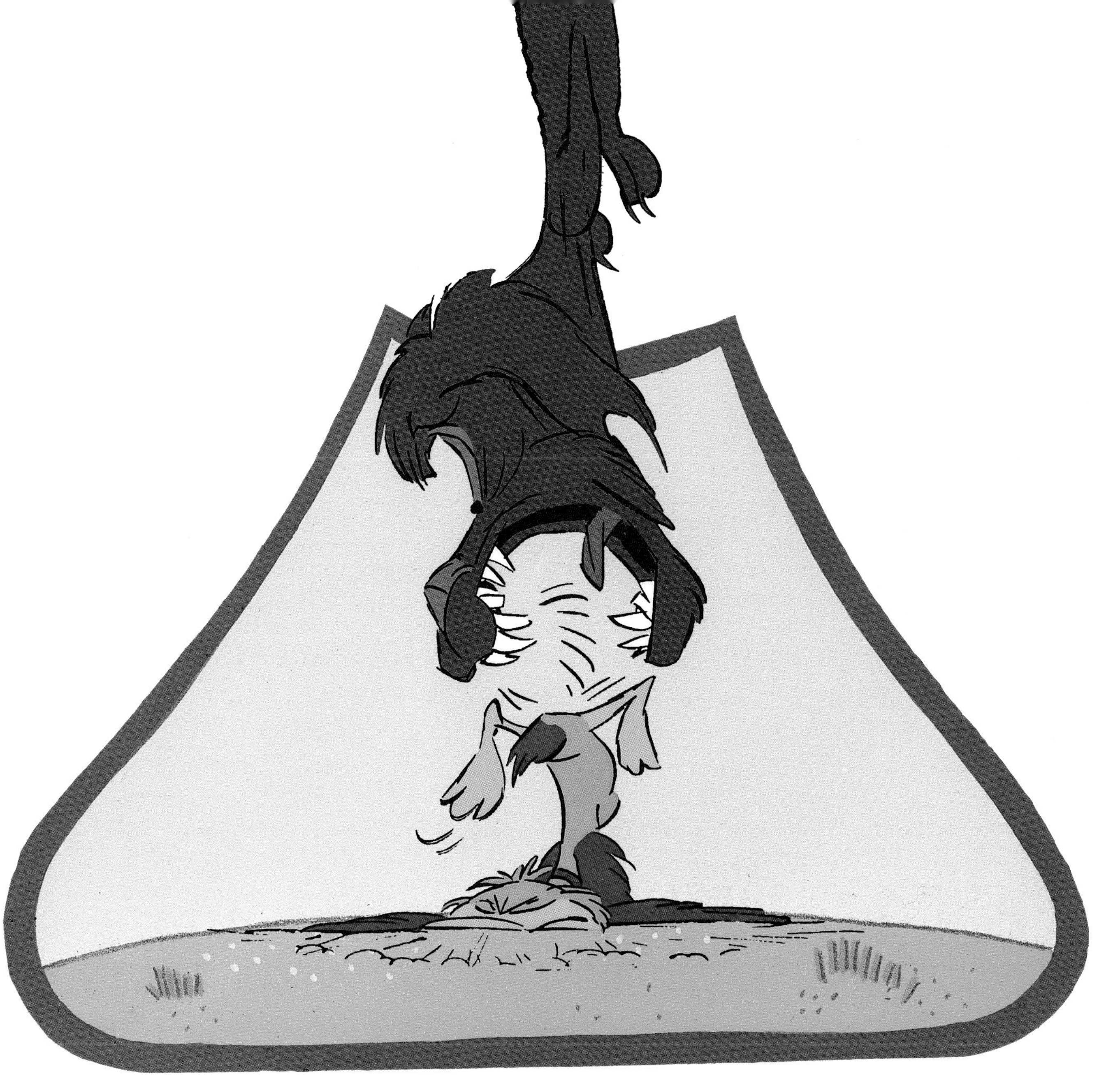

The noise startled the wolf so much that he opened his mouth in surprise and gasped—
and "QUACK!", the duck, still alive, fell out with a KERPLUNK!

Surprised and startled, the hunters drew their guns,

not sure whether to shoot the wolf—or the duck.

"Hey, what are you doing?" cried Peter.

"Don't shoot—ANYTHING!"

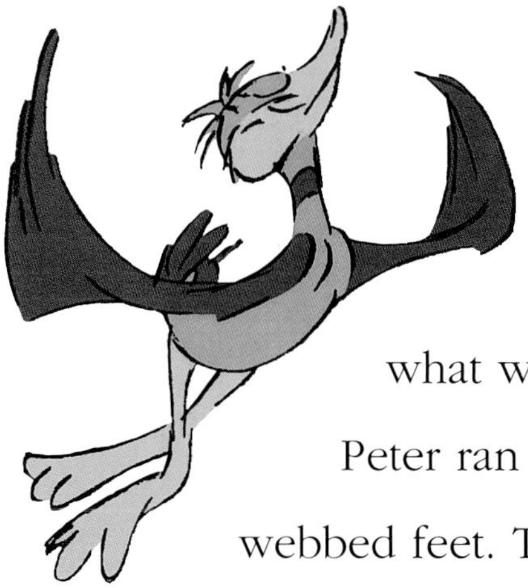

Then he shinned down the tree. The hunters eyes' moved quizzically from side to side as they attempted to figure out exactly what was going on.

Peter ran over and helped the poor, woozy duck get back on his wobbly, webbed feet. The as-always-confused duck, still startled at the turn of events, tried to regain his balance. Instead, though, he merely stumbled giddily around in an incredible combination of hilarious missteps.

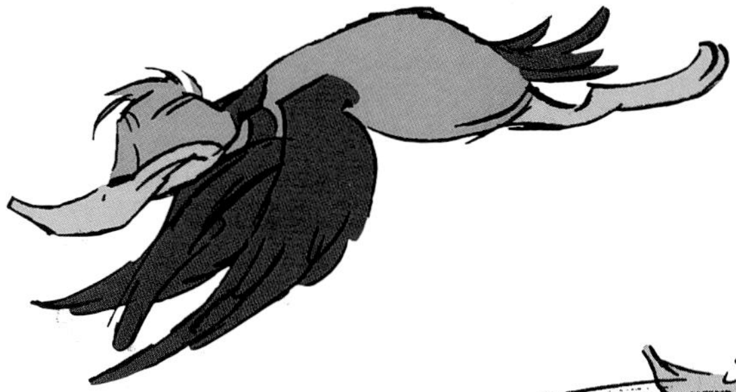

In a flash, the duck realized his extraordinary good luck, what with being resurrected from the pit of the wolf's dark innards. To celebrate, he began to dance around with sheer joy. It was almost as if the duck were performing a ballet of blissful happiness.

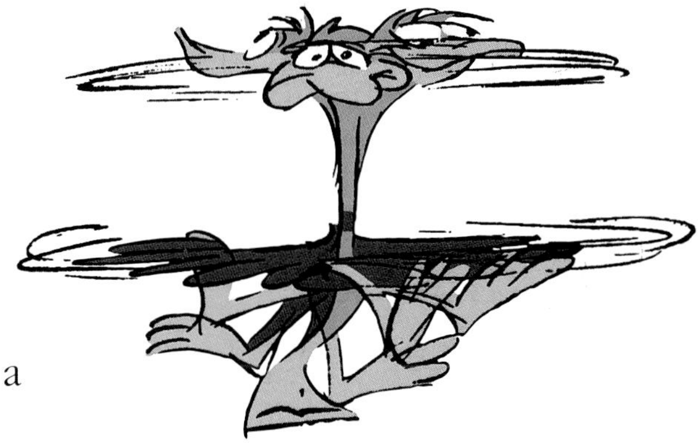

What a whimsical dance it was. The duck glided gleefully around Peter and the bumbling hunters, throwing in a couple of *grands jetés* and pirouettes just for good measure.

But, the duck was still incredibly clumsy, no matter how good his choreographic intentions were. His flailing feet landed him squarely in front of the wolf, still hung up by his tail.

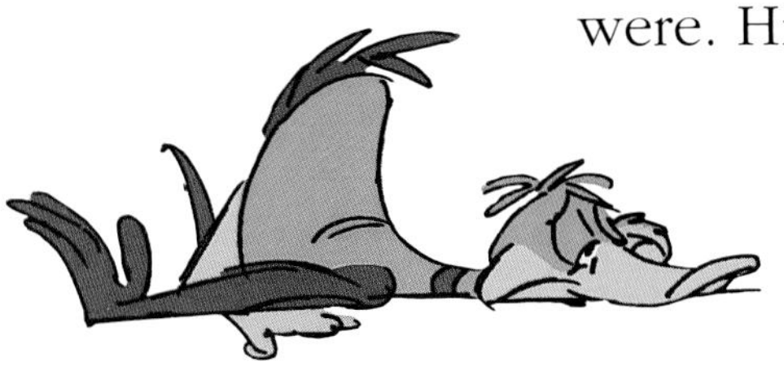

The wolf was now feeling more than a bit mortified at his situation. The duck's wobbly pirouettes didn't help any, either.

"Grrrrrr . . . !!!!" The wolf snapped, and caught the poor duck's tail feathers in his mouth.

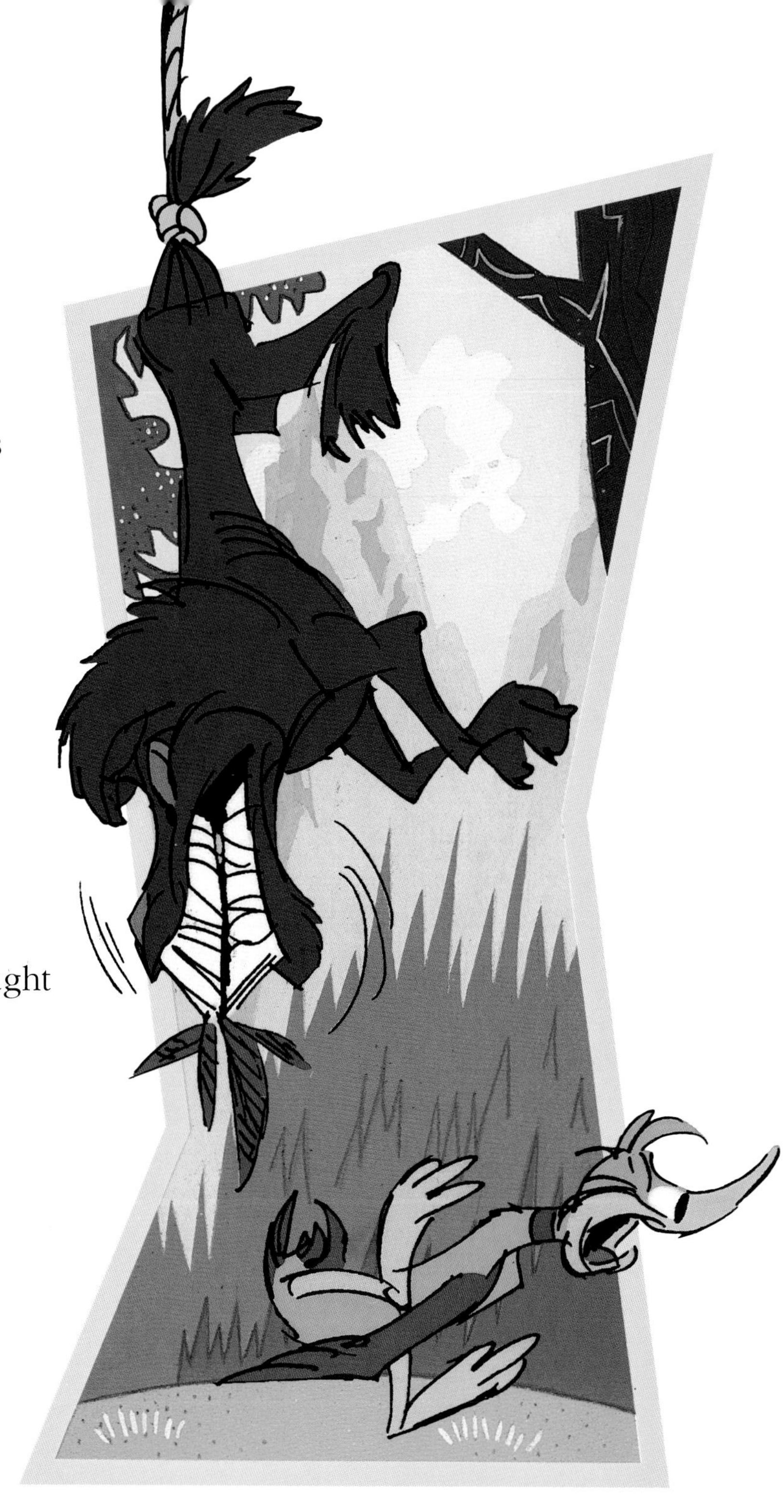

"Oh, no!" Peter cried. But before Peter could make a move, the duck wiggled free on his own and waddled dizzily away, shivering and quivering in fear. He scurried into the tall grass with an agility and lightning-speed that was unusual for him. The duck decided that one brush with a wolf's stomach was enough for a single day.

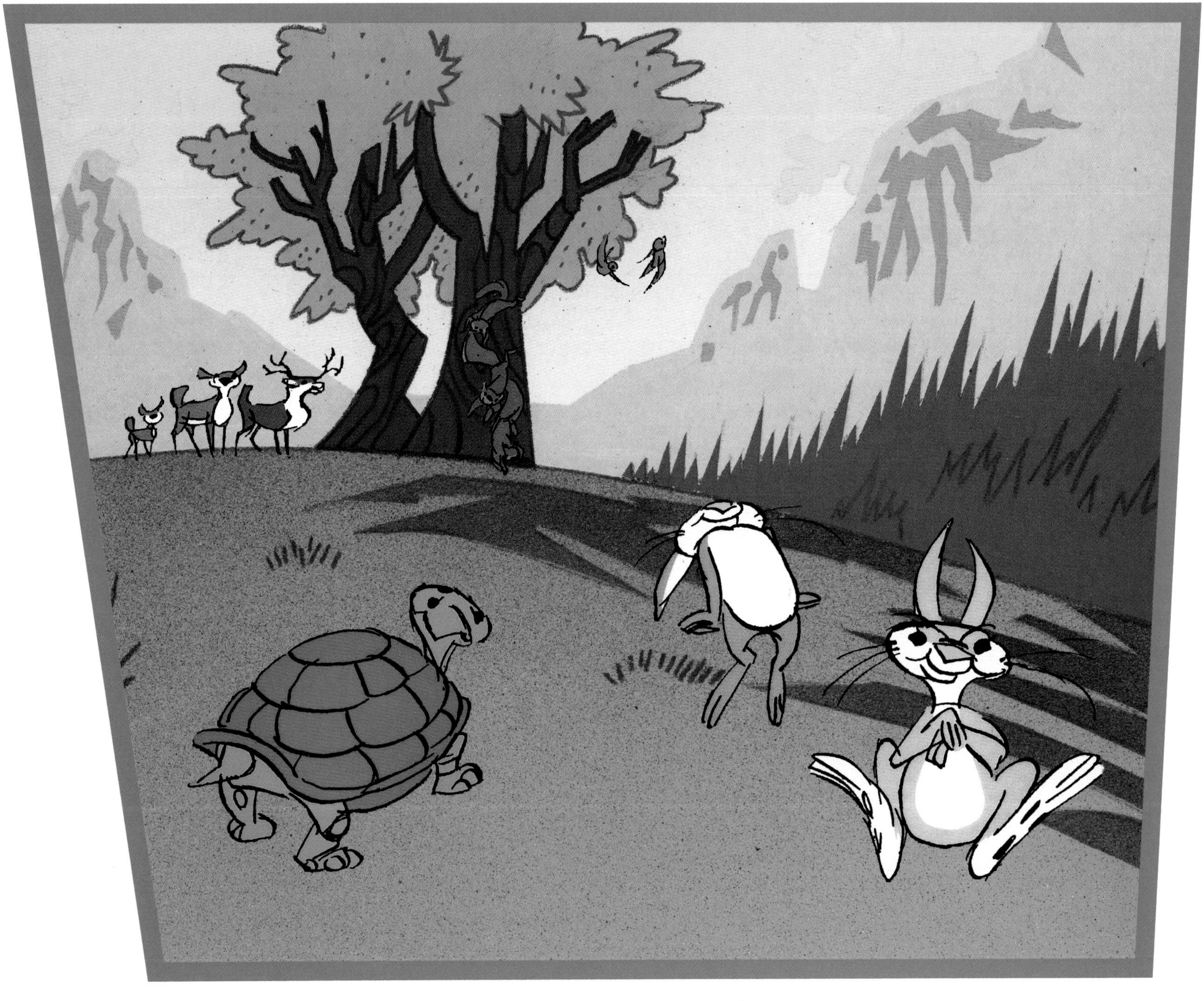

Now Peter took complete charge. "Help us take the wolf to the zoo!" he told the hunters. "You see, the wolf will be safe at the zoo, and so will everyone else!" he explained.

A cheer went up from the hunters and a breeze of relief stirred through the leaves of the meadow. The golden afternoon light filtered playfully through the trees. Once again, the

meadow radiated with happiness as its inhabitants came out from their hiding places. And following Peter's lead, the entire meadow began to prepare for a grand procession to the zoo.

The cat jumped down from the tree, and took his place—proudly—at Peter's side. After all, if it hadn't been for him . . .

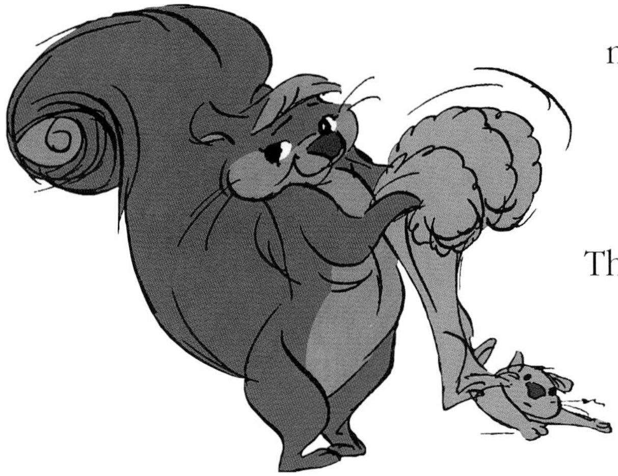

Meanwhile, all over the meadow, preparations were being made for the big event. The mother squirrel fluffed out her babies' tails, and the deer brushed the leaves and grass from their precious fawn.

The rabbit made a wreath of berries and ivy for his bunny-friend. The porcupine sharpened his quills—just in case the wolf got away again. The ladybug wrapped herself in a shimmering gossamer gown of morning glory petals.

And the waterfall sent a joyful cascade of sparkling water straight up in the air, so everyone, for miles around, would know about Peter's fantastic victory in the meadow.

Yes, it was a day to end all days, and at the center of it all stood a proud and beaming Peter.

And a very depressed wolf, still dangling from the tree.

The hunters decided to build a cage for the wolf—

otherwise, how would they get him to the zoo!

They scurried, and scavenged, and searched for enough sticks and twigs to do the job, and used some of Peter's famous rope to tie it all together. Unfortunately, they weren't any better at carpentry than they were at hunting, and the whole affair took on a capricious air of befuddled uncertainty, as everyone else watched in amusement.

Finally, the hunters' determination paid off, and the cage was built. However, getting the wolf in the cage was almost disastrous, for the wolf had other ideas. But, after much shouting and yelling and pushing this way and pulling that, the task was accomplished, and the poor, misunderstood wolf (or so he thought) hung his head in disbelief as his cage was wheeled off to the zoo.

The meadow had never seen anything like this . . . so much excitement, so much celebration, everyone lining up to march to the zoo in the most glorious parade that had ever been seen on this side of the Matterhorn.

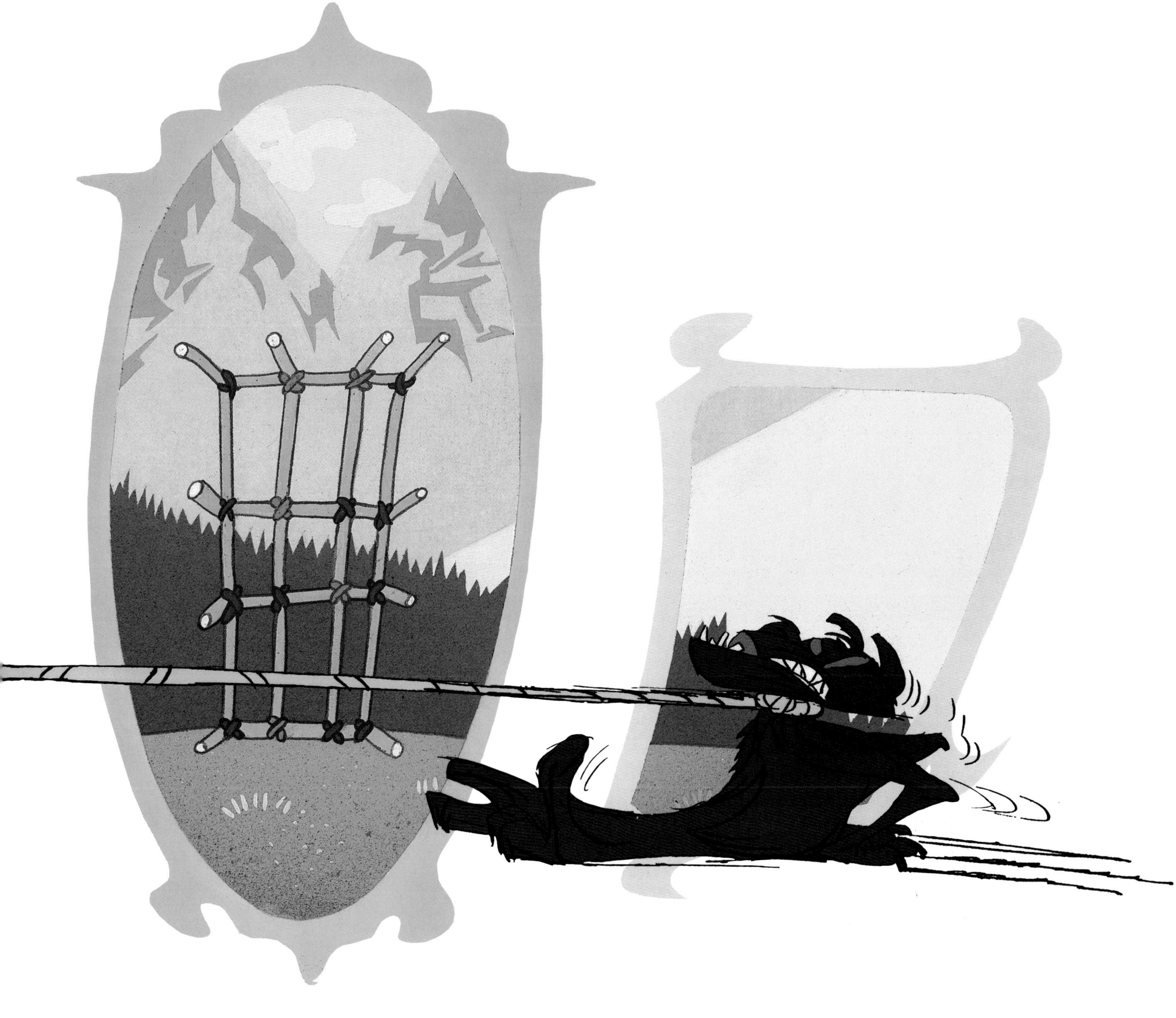

And just when the shouting and the jubilance reached a deafening fever pitch, a loud and unexpected bang resounded across the meadow. And suddenly, everyone—Peter included—fell silent.

For, with a loud whack of the big wooden gate, Grandfather had reappeared.

• • •

All eyes were on Grandfather as he quickly walked across the meadow toward Peter, who was now shifting back and forth in his little boots, looking less like the conquering hero and more like a little boy who had been caught red-handed.

“So, Peter. You disobeyed me again, didn’t you?” the old man said to his grandson.

“But, we . . . but . . . I . . .” He stammered, but then instantly regained his confidence.

“I caught the wolf, didn’t I?”

“Yes, you did. But what would have happened if you hadn’t caught the wolf? What if the wolf had caught you instead?” Grandfather replied.

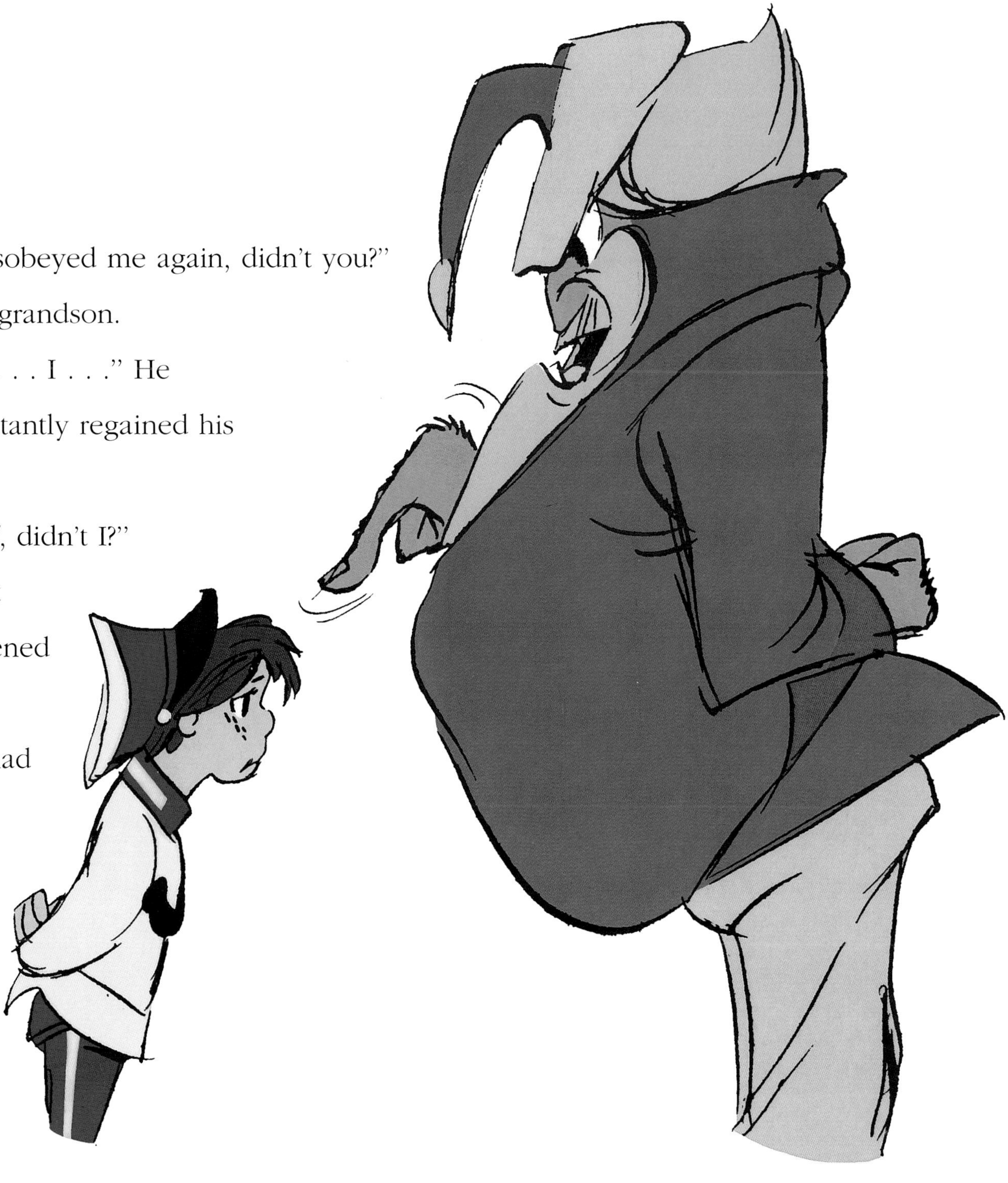

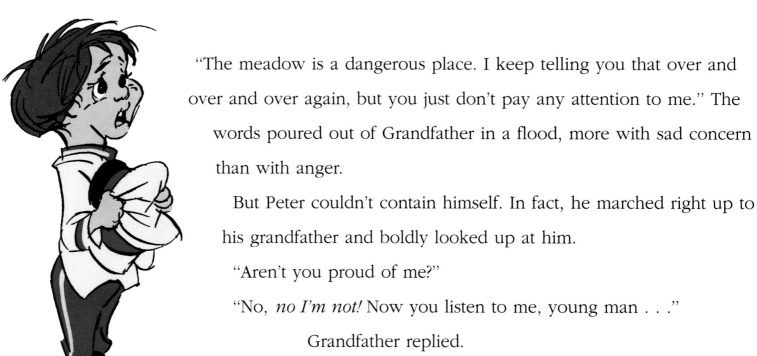

"The meadow is a dangerous place. I keep telling you that over and over and over again, but you just don't pay any attention to me." The words poured out of Grandfather in a flood, more with sad concern than with anger.

But Peter couldn't contain himself. In fact, he marched right up to his grandfather and boldly looked up at him.

"Aren't you proud of me?"

"No, *no I'm not!* Now you listen to me, young man . . ." Grandfather replied.

Peter was wounded, and interrupted Grandfather's tirade.

"Even a little?" Peter spoke in a hush.

Grandfather just gazed at Peter. For the first time, Grandfather realized that, perhaps, his beloved little grandson wasn't such a little boy anymore. He was growing up, and just like the meadow in spring, he was blossoming and blooming and growing with the passing seasons.

"Well, yes, maybe . . . well, maybe a little," Grandfather said quietly. And with those words, an unmistakable gleam appeared in his eye. And on his wrinkled, weathered face, you could see a tiny smile start to break through the clouds of anger that had been there just a few seconds before.

"Well, Peter, yes I am. I am a little proud of you."

Peter smiled and Grandfather continued.

"Actually, maybe even a lot!" Grandfather lovingly beamed.

"C'mon, Grandfather. It won't be a real parade without you!" Peter said, grabbing the old man's shirtsleeve as he led him into the procession.

"I love you, Peter. I really do!" Grandfather said.

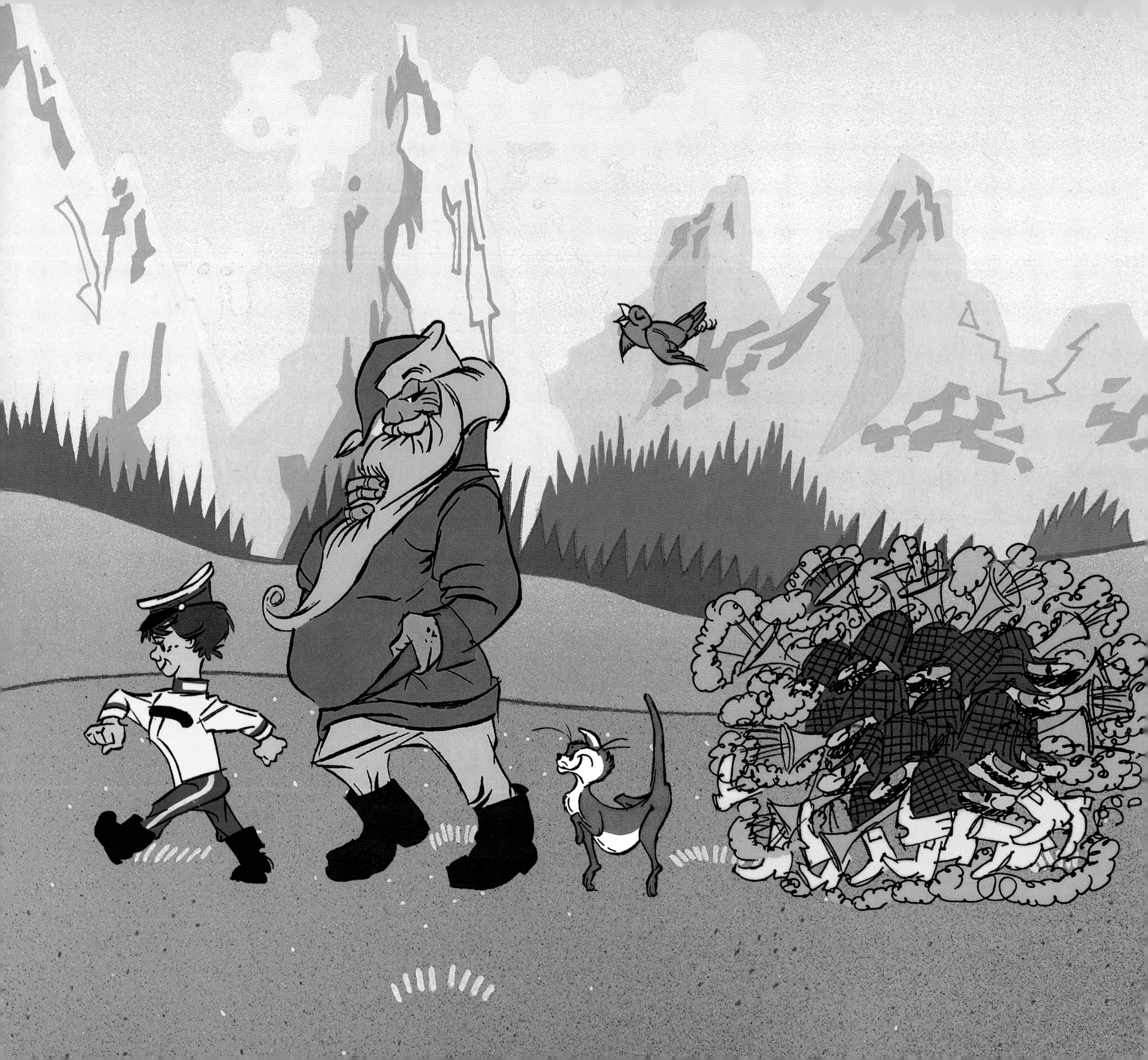

So now, imagine the triumphant parade. Everyone was marching in it, proud of the brave Peter.

And, of course, the bird joined in, too. Not only was she celebrating the wolf's capture, but also her six new babies, who had hatched amid all of the excitement.

Now, following the lead of their mother, this squadron of little birds joyfully flew in front of the parade, leading the way like an airborne honor guard.

Leading Peter and Grandfather.

And the cat.

And the hunters, pulling the wolf's cage. And all the rest of the meadow's happy inhabitants.

Everyone marching. Everyone shouting congratulations at Peter. Everyone celebrating.

Everyone celebrating, that is, except for the duck.

Still shaking with fear, the duck could barely walk, much less march in an important parade. Instead, he stood hiding in the grass, where he trembled all by himself.

"Hey! What are you doing over there?" said Peter as he discovered the duck quivering all alone in a bank of tall reeds.

The duck could only manage a pitiful reply of halfhearted clucks and faint quacks.

Peter gently smoothed his friend's ruffled feathers and did his very best to calm the duck's frayed nerves.

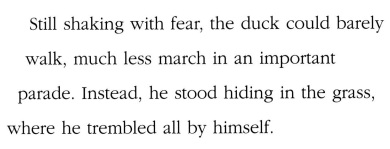

"Listen, you'll never have to be scared again, because I'll always be here to protect you," said Peter.

And with that, Peter gently picked the duck up from the ground, placed him in the honored position on his shoulder, and off they went to join the others.

"What a great first day of spring!" Peter exclaimed.

"Quack!" the duck answered merrily.

The End.

© 1983 Yousuf Karsh

CHUCK JONES is one of the most celebrated directors in the history of animation, and his Warner Bros. masterpieces starring Bugs Bunny, Daffy Duck, Pepé Le Pew, Wile E. Coyote, and the Road Runner (among others) have taken their rightful place among America's most cherished treasures.

In a career that has spanned over 60 years, Jones has made over 250 films, won three Academy Awards, and has been nominated for six others. Jones' razor-sharp eye for character movement, his legendary sense of timing, and his beguilingly irreverent wit have combined to create some of the classic cartoons of all time, including *What's Opera, Doc?, The Rabbit of Seville, One Froggy Evening, Bully for Bugs,* and *For Sentimental Reasons.* Mr. Jones also created and directed *Dr. Seuss' How the Grinch Stole Christmas* and *Horton Hears a Who.*

Chuck Jones has been honored with nine Academy Award nominations, a Museum of Modern Art retrospective, two honorary degrees, and countless honors. His cartoon short *What's Opera, Doc?* recently took its place in the National Archives next to a select, honored group of other great American film masterpieces.

In 1994, Mr. Jones returned to Warner Bros., where his new theatrical animated short *Chariots of Fur* will be released this year as the first in a whole new series of cartoon classics which will not only star his time-honored ensemble of indefatigable animated actors, but some new characters, as well.

Photo by Vera Anderson

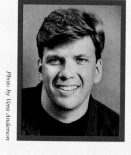

GEORGE DAUGHERTY, writer and creator of this production of *Peter and the Wolf,* is a multi-faceted artist whose professional background includes major credits as a conductor, composer, film and television director, writer, and now, creator of interactive projects.

Daugherty has conducted performances for The Los Angeles Philharmonic, American Ballet Theatre, and The Munich State Opera, among many world-class ensembles. In 1993, he created, wrote, and directed *Rhythm & Jam,* a series of kids' music specials for ABC, which was honored with multiple Emmy Award nominations. In that same year, he also directed *The Magical World of Chuck Jones,* a film honoring the great animation director on his 80th birthday, featuring interviews with Whoopi Goldberg, Steven Spielberg, George Lucas, Ron Howard, and 20 other stars.

He has composed animation scores for Warner Bros. and the major television networks, has been honored with three Emmy nominations, and most recently co-composed the score for Chuck Jones' new Warner Bros. theatrical short *Chariots of Fur.* In 1990, he created Warner Bros. *Bugs Bunny on Broadway,* which took New York by storm in a held-over run at The Gershwin Theatre, and is still touring throughout the world.

Photo by Yervand Mikailian

JANIS DIAMOND, an Emmy Award-nominated writer, has written for *Sesame Street, The Electric Company, Land of the Lost, Sonic the Hedgehog,* and *The Adventure of Raggedy Ann and Andy,* which she also developed for television. As a ground-breaking writer for the interactive CD-ROM medium, she has written numerous titles, including the highly acclaimed *Girls' Club* and the just-released *Where in the World Is Carmen Sandiego, Jr.?*